D0822055

EDINBURGH
STEP BY STEP
Guided walks around Scotland's Capital

Christopher Turner

HarperCollins*Publishers*

HarperCollins*Publishers*
Westerhill Road, Bishopbriggs, Glasgow G64 2QT

First published 2000

Reprint 10 9 8 7 6 5 4 3 2 1 0

© Text and photographs: Christopher Turner, 2000
© Cartography: Draughtsman Limited, Southam Street, London, 2000

ISBN 0 00 472346-5

A catalogue record for this book is available from the British Library

Every effort has been made to provide an up-to-date text but the publishers
cannot accept any liability for errors, omissions or changes in detail or for
any consequences arising from the use of information contained herein. The
publishers welcome corrections and suggestions from readers. Write to:

Reference Department
HarperCollins*Publishers*
Westerhill Road
Bishopbriggs
Glasgow G64 2QT

CONTENTS

Other Collins Scottish Titles

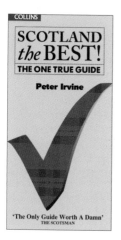

Scotland the Best!
(ISBN 0 00 472399-6, priced £12.99)

Edinburgh the Best!
(ISBN 0 00 472464-X, priced £6.99)

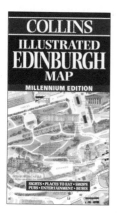

Illustrated Edinburgh Map
(ISBN 0 00 448944-6, priced £3.50)

INTRODUCTION

Although compact, Edinburgh's centre is so packed with interest that to explore it thoroughly takes a considerable amount of time, much of which can be wasted searching for easy-to-miss locations. *Edinburgh Step by Step,* with its uniquely precise directions, combined with clear maps, ensures that nothing will be missed, and that the visitor will not get lost or go round in circles.

The city is divided into eleven itineraries, most of which interlink. Over 150 major locations are covered and, after giving a brief history, the visitor is led, literally step by step, around the exterior and, when appropriate, the interior of each one. Every point of interest is referred to precisely as it is reached, and directions are then given for continuing to the next location. In other words, *Edinburgh Step by Step* aims to match as closely as possible the services of a personal, knowledgeable guide.

Cost savings to the reader can be significant: reduced time spent sightseeing, no additional street maps or guidebooks, no personal guides, lower transport charges.

With the recent opening to visitors of major attractions such as Dynamic Earth, the Royal Yacht *Britannia* and the Museum of Scotland, now, more than ever, is the time to make a first or a return visit to this serenely picturesque capital city.

Edinburgh Castle

❖ Open daily April to October 9.30am to 6pm. November to March 11am to 5pm. ❖ Admission charge includes the hire of a 4-hour audio guide, and regular guide services.

Now primarily an ancient monument, Edinburgh Castle was built as a residence for the royal family that could be defended from attack. It is not only Scotland's most popular tourist attraction, but also its national symbol. The complex houses Scotland's Crown Jewels and National War Memorial and, although the castle is no longer a military fortress, it provides barracks for a limited number of troops, together with regimental museums.

Castle Rock, the great mound of basalt resulting from an extinct volcano on which the castle stands, completely dominates Grassmarket to the north and Princes Street to the south. Most visitors to Scotland's capital gain their first sight of Castle Rock as they exit from Waverley Station, and are immediately overwhelmed by its grandeur.

Edinburgh Castle from the Balmoral Hotel

History

Recent Bronze-Age finds confirm a 2nd-century settlement on Castle Hill, but a feast attended by the Gododdi war band and their leader King Mynyddog Mwynfawr at Din Eidyn ('stronghold of Eidyn') in the 6th century seems to be the first known reference to the castle. The only structure to predate the 15th century is the 12th-century St Margaret's Chapel.

Between 1296 and 1341 the Scots fought the English for their independence, and the castle changed hands four times, during which the defences were dismantled, rebuilt and extended. David II began major reconstruction in 1356, but of his work only the ruined base of David's Tower has survived. In 1433, the King's Great Chamber was built to link with the royal apartment in David's Tower, but

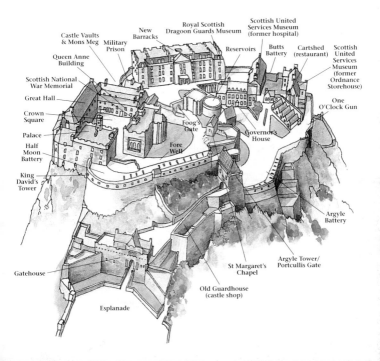

had to be rebuilt after the siege of 1445. Ten years later, James III laid out a road to the summit that could be used by artillery; he also built a furnace, which marked the start of the gradual transition of the castle from a royal residence to an ordnance factory.

By the 1530s, so many buildings on the summit had been adapted for either the manufacture or storage of weaponry that Edinburgh Castle no longer provided an agreeable royal residence. After the death of James V in 1542, the Scottish monarchy, not surprisingly, vacated the castle for the Palace of Holyroodhouse, where Scottish kings had resided periodically for many years.

Many opposed the enforced abdication of Mary, Queen of Scots, including Sir William Kirkcaldy of Grange, Keeper of Edinburgh Castle, which resulted in the Lang Siege (1571–73). Not until Regent Morton gained the support of the English did the siege come to an end: heavy guns from six batteries bombarded the east end of the castle, and its defences, including the 14th-century David's and Constable towers, collapsed. After the garrison had surrendered, Regent Morton commissioned the rebuilding of the eastern defences.

From now on, the castle was given over entirely to the military, and most of its buildings, including the palace and the vaults, would be converted to barracks. In 1617, however, James VI visited Edinburgh, and preparations for his 'Hamecoming' included the extension and renovation of the palace, including the tiny 'cabinet' where he had been born.

Charles I was the last reigning monarch to sleep at the castle, the occasion being the night before his coronation as King of Scotland at Holyrood in 1633. In spite of its defences, the castle was successfully besieged by the Covenanters in 1640, Cromwell's Roundheads in 1650 and Bonnie Prince Charlie's Jacobite supporters in 1745.

By the mid-18th century it was accepted that the castle was no longer a fortress. Its status as a national monument began in 1818 with the rediscovery of the Honours (Crown Jewels) of Scotland, which immediately went on show to the public.

In accordance with late 19th-century taste, picturesque but inaccurate restoration of the Great Hall and Portcullis Gate and replacement of the Gatehouse took place. After World War I ended in 1918, it was decided that the castle would no longer accommodate a large body of troops, and vacant barracks were gradually converted to regimental museums. Architectural work of major importance ended in 1927, when the 18th-century North Barracks was remodelled with 'baronial' trappings to become the Scottish National War Memorial.

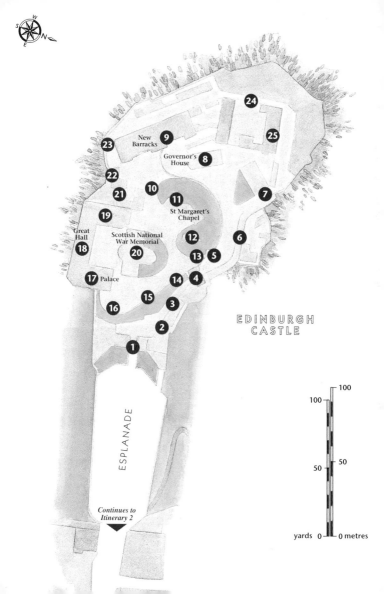

New Barracks

Governor's House

St Margaret's Chapel

Scottish National War Memorial

Great Hall

Palace

EDINBURGH CASTLE

ESPLANADE

Continues to Itinerary 2

100

50

0

100

50

yards 0

0 metres

Castle Tour

Numbered plaques throughout the castle indicate points of greatest interest, and the suggested route described in this book follows them in sequence; numbers shown correlate with each plaque.

Esplanade

Created in 1753 as a parade ground, the Esplanade was widened and embellished by its present low wall and north railings 1816–20. In the summer of 1947, to coincide with the city's first International Festival, a military display was given on the Esplanade every evening: the event proved so popular that it has been repeated annually. Known as the Edinburgh Tattoo, pipes and drummers march and counter-march before the romantic backdrop of the illuminated castle. The Esplanade also provides a platform for Edinburgh's great firework displays, which signal the end of each Festival – and the beginning of a new year.

➠ *Proceed to the castle's entrance.*

Gatehouse   1

A relatively small, unimpressive gate erected by Cromwell around 1690 was replaced by the present, more flamboyant structure, with its bridge, 1886–88. Bronze figures set beneath Gothic-style canopies represent Scottish heroes Robert the Bruce and Sir William Wallace, both added in 1929. Above the arch are the arms of Regent Morton, the vigorous opponent of Mary, Queen of Scots. Within the arch have been set 17th-century carvings of artillery, including the famous siege gun (bombard) Mons Meg. The gatehouse leads to the relatively small Lower Ward, the first of the castle's three levels.

➠ *Continue ahead to the shop, right.*

Old Guardhouse/Castle Shop   2

Constructed in 1853 to replace a guardhouse of 1801, this building was extended thirteen years later by the addition of detention cells.

Inner Barrier   3

Beside the entrance to the Old Guardhouse, two gate piers are all that survive of the early 19th-century inner barrier.

A plaque high up on the wall, left, commemorates Sir William Kirkcaldy, keeper of Edinburgh Castle, which he defended on behalf of Mary, Queen of Scots throughout the Lang Siege of 1571–73.

Portcullis Gate   4   ## Argyle Tower   13

What was left of the cylindrical Constable's Tower after the Lang Siege served as a base for the present Portcullis Gate, completed in 1577. It was not then, as at present, surmounted by the two-storey tower, which was added in 1584, primarily to provide cover for a replacement portcullis, the original having rusted. Its upper floor was rebuilt in 1887 by Hippolyte Blanc as a reproduction of the lost Constable's Tower. The tower's name commemorates Archibald, 9th Earl of Argyle, who is said to have been imprisoned in the tower prior to his execution in 1685.

 Proceed through the gateway to the Middle Ward. Passed immediately left is a steep flight of steps, which ascends to the Upper Ward.

Lang Stairs   5

Until James III improved the road from here to the summit in 1464, stairs at this point provided the main access to the Upper Ward. Although now relatively modern, these 72 steps follow the medieval route and still offer the shortest, albeit the steepest, way of reaching the summit.

The wall, right, that curves around the base of the stairs may be the remains of a medieval tower.

Foundations of the 1801 guardhouse ahead, left, are now surrounded by display boards. Facing them is one of the castle's principal batteries.

Argyle Battery   6

The six-gun battery, on a raised platform fronted by a castellated wall, protects the north flank of the castle. It was a replacement battery of the 1730s but the present guns were made for the Napoleonic Wars of the early 19th century; each is a cast iron, muzzle-loaded 18-pounder. From this point there is a wide panorama of the New Town.

➠ *Continue right to the Mills Mount Battery.*

Cartshed (and 'One O'clock Gun')   7

Standing in splendid isolation on Mills Mount Battery, the World War II 25-pounder gun is fired Monday to Saturday at 1pm. The tradition began in 1861, inspired by the toy gun in the garden of the Palais Royal in Paris. Initially, a 64-pounder muzzle-loaded gun was fired from the Half Moon Battery, the efforts of four men being required to operate it; the present gun can be fired by one man. Only for brief periods during both world wars was the custom suspended.

Cartshed, now a café/restaurant for visitors, was originally built around 1746 as a series of pedimented, open-fronted hangars, which could shelter up to fifty carts loaded with provisions.

➠ *Bear left, passing the pair of trees, right, to the solid Georgian house, with matching north and south wings.*

Governor's House   8

This typically Georgian building was designed in 1742 as a five-bay official residence for the Castle Governor, with side wings for the Master Governor and the Storekeeper. In 1860, the position of governor became redundant, and his residence was assigned to sisters of the castle's hospital; it now serves as the Officers' Mess. Since 1935, a governor has been appointed once more, but directly by the Crown and with only a ceremonial role; the north wing is now reserved for his use.

At the south end, steps descend to the regimental museum of the Royal Scots Dragoon Guards.

➠ *Proceed to the castle's south-west corner.*

New Barracks   9

Until this barracks for 600 personnel was completed in 1796, the garrison's troops had been inadequately accommodated in the Great Hall. It now serves various military purposes.

Facing the south end of the building, the museum of the Royal Scots Regiment occupies the Drill Hall, built in 1900.

➡ *Proceed to the east side of the quadrangle facing the New Barracks and follow the path that curves uphill through the archway.*

Foog's Gate   10

Although this was the main entrance to the Upper Ward of the castle, it is not known when the gate was first built nor how it gained its name; the present structure, with its perimeter wall, dates from the reign of Charles II (1649–85). Ahead, the bookshop occupies a fire station built in late 19th-century 'medieval' style.

Upper Ward

This, the highest and most important part of the castle, lies on the east side of the gate. To provide a greater building area, much of the natural rock has been removed or built up through the centuries.

➡ *Continue ahead to the castle's oldest building, left.*

St Margaret's Chapel   11

This small Romanesque chapel is the only part of the castle to survive Robert the Bruce's dismantling of 1314. It appears to have been built by David I (1124–53), the younger son of Queen Margaret, who had died within the castle in 1093. Margaret was not canonized until 1250, and the chapel could not therefore have been dedicated to her until after that date. For centuries the building was believed to have been demolished, but it was rediscovered in 1845, serving as a storehouse. Restoration was completed in 1852, when the chapel was reopened for worship, and the adjacent garrison chapel demolished.

Externally, the small building is plain and severe. Seen first, the round-arched window on the east side is original but those in the south and west walls have been renewed. The design of the roof indicates that it was rebuilt in the 18th century.

➡ *Enter by the north door (created in 1939).*

The nave's tunnel vault is 19th-century restoration work, but most of the chancel arch is early 12th-century. Typically Romanesque, the arch has a chevron (dog tooth) pattern. Although the four shafts are 1852 replacements, their scallop capitals are original. All the chapel's stained-glass windows were made by Douglas Strachan in 1922: depicted in the chancel are St Andrew and St Ninian, and in the nave St Columba, St Margaret and Sir William Wallace. A copy of St Margaret's gospel book is displayed in the chapel; the original is in the Bodleian Library, Oxford.

➠ *Exit left, and continue ahead to the castle's north wall.*

Dog Cemetery   12

Below the wall, the small garden has been used since around 1840 as a burial ground for dogs that had been regimental mascots or officers' pets. Its curved parapet was built in the 18th century, apparently around the stump of a medieval tower.

➠ *Follow the wall of the Upper Ward clockwise, passing the Lang Stairs and the roof of the Argyle Tower (13) to the next battery.*

Forewall Battery   14

The line of this 17th-century battery is believed to follow that of a medieval pre-decessor. Its present guns were made around 1810.

➠ *Follow the east wall to the end of the battery.*

Fore Well   15

Since the 19th century, all parts of Edinburgh Castle have been supplied with water from the city below; prior to this, wells inside the castle were the only practical source. The circular Fore Well supplied most of the Upper Ward's water from the early 14th century, but its limited capacity of 2,240 gallons (11,135 litres) was hardly sufficient for the castle's garrison to withstand a siege of much length. When St David's Tower collapsed during the 1573 bombardment, rubble from its upper storeys blocked the well, thereby necessitating the surrender of the garrison.

West of the Fore Well protrudes the polygonal apse and east arm of the Scottish National War Memorial, visited later.

➠ *Continue southward to the castle's most important battery.*

The Edinburgh Tattoo

Half Moon Battery | 16

After David's Tower had been destroyed in the 1573 siege, Regent Morton ordered the immediate construction over its remains of the Half Moon Battery, so-named due to its shape; it was completed in 1588. The present guns are early 19th-century 18-pounders. Every performance of the Edinburgh Tattoo on the Esplanade below ends, movingly, with a lone piper playing from this battery.

▥▶ *Descend the slope, turn left and proceed beneath the arch to Crown Square, the historic royal core of Edinburgh Castle.*

Crown Square

In the reign of James III (1460–88), it was decided that the castle's royal accommodation, both state and private, would be reconstructed. Built facing the medieval St Mary's Chapel was the Great Hall; east of this the Palace and, to the west, the Kitchens and Gunhouse: a quadrangle, to be known as Palace Yard, was thereby created. Castle Rock sloped abruptly southward and, to maximise the space available, a flat platform supported by stone vaults was created.

▥▶ *Proceed to the Royal Palace, on the east side of the square.*

Royal Palace   17

Although the Palace was built in the second half of the 15th century, it appears to have incorporated the Great Chamber of 1433, which was linked with David's Tower. Little 15th-century work apart from the fabric has survived, much of the building having been remodelled for the brief return visit to Edinburgh of James VI in 1617 (the king's 'Hamecoming').

West front of the Palace

The upper floor replaced most of an existing attic in 1617, providing four storeys north of the stair tower and three storeys south of it. The stair tower was originally given a lead ogee (onion-shaped) roof, but this was lost in 1820 when the structure was raised by two storeys and its clock installed. The south end of the Palace retains its former attic floor. Here, above the round-arched doorway, a stone panel is inscribed with the MAH (Mary And Henry) monogram of Mary, Queen of Scots and her second husband, Henry, Lord Darnley; its 1566 date commemorates the birth, in a small room within, of their son, James VI. The entire west front of the Palace is severely plain but, as will be seen, its east front, which overlooks Old Town, is more ambitious.

➡ *Return beneath the arch to Half Moon Battery and proceed to its south end.*

East front of the Palace

To distinguish the royal apartments, created in 1617, finely cut and pointed blocks of stone (ashlar) were used rather than the stone rubble employed elsewhere. Gilded decoration above the three upper and two lower windows incorporate crowns, swags of fruit, the date 1616 and the monogram of James VI, IR6 (Iacobus Rex 6). Between the top three windows are two framed panels; one features the Honours of Scotland, the other, now blank, displayed the royal arms until removed by Cromwell in 1652.

➡ *Return towards Crown Square.*

North front of the Palace

This stone-rubble front is centrally divided by an ogee-roofed stair tower, which probably resembles the former appearance of that on the east front. Here also, the pediments above the windows of the royal apartments are decorated with royal insignia.

➡ *Continue beneath the arch to Crown Square, turn left and enter the palace from its central stair tower. Ascend to the Honours of the Kingdom Exhibition, which incorporates the regalia and the Stone of Destiny.*

Honours of the Kingdom Exhibition

The history of Scotland's royal regalia and Stone of Destiny is   depicted by tableaux.

Stone of Destiny

The Stone of Destiny (or of Scone) served as the 'throne' on which Scottish kings were crowned between the 9th and 13th centuries. In 1296 the English King Edward I appropriated the stone, which was kept beneath the Coronation Chair (specially made for it) at Westminster Abbey. All English and British sovereigns have been crowned seated above the Stone of Destiny ever since. The stone was returned to Scotland by Queen Elizabeth II in 1996, and is kept at the castle.

Honours of Scotland

Unlike the Crown Jewels of England, Scotland's were saved from the clutches of Oliver Cromwell, who would undoubtedly have sold them as well. Just before Edinburgh Castle fell to the Roundheads in 1650, the regalia was taken to Dunnottar Castle, and thence, after its capture, smuggled out by the wife of the minister of nearby Kinneff Church, accompanied by her maid, and buried beneath the floor of the building. On the restoration of Charles II in 1660, the Honours of Scotland were returned to Edinburgh Castle.

The Crown Room, in which the regalia is displayed, was built as a strong room specifically to house it in 1617. The coronation of Charles II at Scone in 1651 (two years after the execution of his father Charles I, and nine years before his enthronement at Westminster Abbey) was the last occasion on which the regalia would be used at such ceremonies.

In 1707, following the Act of Union between England and Scotland, the door of the Crown Room was walled up. In 1818, writer Sir Walter Scott persuaded the Prince Regent to issue a royal warrant to reopen the room; within it a chest was prized open and the Honours of Scotland were rediscovered. Following this event, Palace Yard was renamed Crown Square.

The regalia, together with the Stone of Destiny, is displayed in a glass showcase.

Sword of State

Domenico da Sutri made the sword, with its scabbard and belt, for Pope Julius II, who presented it to James IV in 1507. They are exquisite examples of Italian Renaissance craftsmanship.

Crown

James V commissioned Edinburgh goldsmith John Mosman to produce a more impressive crown for him to wear at the coronation of his second consort, Mary of Guise, in 1540. Mosman melted down the existing crown, added Scottish gold from Upper Clydesdale and incorporated a further 23 precious stones. Interestingly, the high-arched (imperial) form of the previous crown, made for James III (1460–88), resembled closely that of the crown spire of St Giles Cathedral, which was built during the same period, and some believe that the design of one of them may have influenced that of the other. On 1 July 1999 the crown was placed in front of Queen Elizabeth II at the first session of the new Scottish Parliament.

Sceptre

Around 1494, Pope Alexander VI presented James IV with the silver gilt sceptre which, like the sword, was made in Renaissance Italy. In 1536, James V commissioned Andrew Leys, an Edinburgh goldsmith, to lengthen it and produce a more elaborate finial.

Regalia connected with the Orders of the Garter and the Thistle are displayed separately in a wall case.

➡ *Descend the steps to the Royal Apartment.*

Queen Mary's Chambers

Following the death of her first husband, François II of France, Mary, Queen of Scots returned to Scotland, and in July 1565 married her cousin Henry Darnley. When she became pregnant, it was decided that for historic reasons the queen's first child should be born at Edinburgh Castle rather than the Palace of Holyroodhouse, where she then resided. Prepared for her sojourn in the castle's palace were the Great Chamber (no longer identifiable), an Inner Chamber and a small anteroom known as the Cabinet, where the future James VI would be born, on 19 June 1566.

Inner Chamber

This larger room displays portraits of the Stuarts.

Cabinet

None of the room's painting existed at the time of James's birth: all of it dates from the 1617 preparations for his 'Hamecoming'. The wooden ceiling, probably 16th-century work, is decorated with thistles, crowns and the initials of the queen and her son – MR (Maria Regina) and IR (Iacobus Rex). Painted on boards at upper wall level are 19 IVNII (19 June), the royal arms of Scotland above a religious inscription invoking Christ's blessing on the House of Stuart, and the date 1566. Wooden panelling below the painted boards was made around 1700 but not installed here until 1848.

Laich Hall

Visitors are shown a suite of reconstructed rooms, one of which, the Laich (low) Hall, was an outer dining room.

In spite of the great expenditure on the Palace to receive the royal couple, James I's consort, Anne of Denmark, did not accompany her husband to Edinburgh and, although the King held court at the castle, he decided to lodge at the Palace of Holyroodhouse.

➡ *Exit left and proceed clockwise around the square.*

Great Hall   18

It seems probable that the hall was built towards the end of the reign of James IV (1488–1513), but it may have been partly constructed, or reconstructed, by James V (1513–42). From 1650 the Great Hall served as a barracks and a military hospital, but in 1887 Hippolyte Blanc was commissioned to restore the building. Over-enthusiastic as ever, he left very few original features 'unimproved'.

Exterior

Blocked rounded arches above the four windows indicate the originals, which were only half the height of Blanc's replacements. Towards the centre, the blocked arch below the window was the 16th-century entrance, which Blanc moved to the west end of the hall and gave a Gothic-style doorway.

➡ *Enter the hall.*

Interior

Although much altered by Blanc, the timber roof remains in essence late medieval, and is one of the grandest of its type in Scotland. The king's principal carpenter, John Drummond, is believed to have been responsible for the work, which is a Scottish version of the English hammerbeam roof. In the late 18th century, possibly in connection with erecting a false ceiling beneath the roof, the ends of the hammerbeams, including their carved beasts decoration, were cut off. Blanc removed the flat Georgian ceiling and made various amendments to the roof, but did not restore its truncated hammerbeams.

The design of the decorated scroll-shaped corbels that support the roof has obviously been influenced by the Renaissance. Some of them are inscribed IR (Iacobus Rex) 4, indicating that the roof dates from the reign of James IV, who was killed at the Battle of Flodden in 1513. However, no other Renaissance architectural motifs in Scotland predate 1530, which has led to suggestions that

Left: Scottish National War Memorial

the roof was constructed or reconstructed for James V, who simply included his father's initials on a corbel to honour him as the builder of its predecessor. Blanc was responsible for the painting of the arms of the governors of the castle on the rafters' corbels.

The remainder of the hall is entirely the work of Blanc, including its 15th-century-style fireplace; the armour is on loan from the Royal Armories.

➠ *Return to Castle Square and proceed, left, to the west range.*

Queen Anne Building | 19

The building, constructed in 1708 (i.e. during the reign of Queen Anne), occupies the site of Cromwell's New Barracks of 1650, which in turn probably replaced the medieval kitchens and Gunhouse. It now serves as a summer café, and provides exhibition space.

➠ *Proceed to the north side of Crown Square.*

Scottish National War Memorial | 20

At the end of World War I (1914–18) it was decided to honour Scots who had lost their lives in the conflict by erecting a national memorial at Edinburgh Castle. On the site had stood St Mary's Church, for centuries the most important royal place of worship in the castle, but in 1540, when Edinburgh Castle had ceased to be a royal residence, it was converted to a munitions store. In 1755, the building was demolished and replaced by the North Barracks. Robert Lorimer was commissioned to convert this to a war memorial in 1923, and both externally and internally the mock-medieval detailing is his. All that survives of the barracks are its rubble stone walls, some of which incorporated material re-used from St Mary's Church.

Crown Square front

Lorimer added the centrally-placed porch and the semicircular steps leading up to it. Round-arched apertures in Romanesque style are combined with Gothic tracery and gargoyles. The insubstantial arch linking the building with the Palace, to its south, has no structural significance.

➡ *Enter the building from the porch.*

Interior

The long aisle, known as the Hall of Honour, accommodates a regimental monument in each north bay. Visitors are given a plan. Facing the porch, behind wrought-iron gates, the apse was added by Lorimer to house the memorial's shrine. Within this, a steel casket presented by George V and Queen Mary contains scrolls inscribed with the names of the 150,000 Scots who fell in World War I. The monument now also commemorates the 50,000 Scots who were killed in World War II (1939–45) and subsequent conflicts. Both end chapels incorporate more regimental monuments against their south-facing walls, and additional monuments are located against columns. Stained glass is the work of Douglas Strachan.

➡ *Exit right and leave Crown Square at its north-west corner, right. Descend the slope through Foog's Gate and turn left. Follow signs to the Castle Vaults and Mons Meg.*

Immediately left is the Royal Scots regimental museum. Charles I founded the 'Royal' regiment in 1633, and its display is the largest in the castle dedicated to a single regiment.

➡ *Continue down the slope, left, passing, right, the HQ of the Royal Scots.*

Castle Vaults   21

When the stone vaults were built in the 15th century to provide a base for a level platform for Castle Square, they were immediately utilised for storage. Subsequently the vaults served as part of the Gunhouse, barracks, a bakehouse and prison cells. Their star attraction now, however, is the enormous siege gun, known as Mons Meg.

➡ *Follow the passage ahead.*

Mons Meg

In 1459, Philip the Good, Duke of Burgundy, presented his nephew James II with two bombards, the largest siege guns ever made. One of them, known as Mons Meg (it was made at Mons in Belgium), has survived.

The gun was muzzle-loaded and able to fire 330 lb (150 kg) gunstones for a distance of at least 2 miles. Unfortunately, Mons Meg weighed more than 6 tons (6096 kg) and could only be wheeled 3 miles (5 km) in a day – on firm, level ground. This was hardly practical, and after 100 years of very limited service, Mons Meg was restricted to firing salutes from the ramparts of Edinburgh Castle. Even this proved too much for the veteran, and in 1681, firing a birthday salute for the future James VII, its barrel burst. Although it was repaired, Mons Meg would never fire again, and the bombard was parked beside Foog's Gate until, in 1754, it was despatched to the Tower of London. Due to the efforts of Sir Walter Scott, Mons Meg was returned to Edinburgh in 1829.

➠ *Proceed to the former prison cells.*

Prison cells

War prisoners of several nationalities, most of them sailors, were incarcerated in these vaults during the 18th and early 19th centuries. In spite of the apparent invulnerability of the vaults, many escaped, including 49 Frenchmen who accomplished a mass break-out in 1811. In addition to prisoners of war, military and civil prisoners were confined in the castle's vaults.

Carved on wood and stone is prisoners' graffito; noteworthy are depictions of the British Prime Minister Lord North being hanged from a gallows, dated 1780 (French), and a ship flying the American flag of independence (American).

➠ *Exit from the vaults and proceed ahead to another former prison.*

Military Prison   22

This prison was purpose-built around 1842 to accommodate miscreants from the castle's garrison. It was extended in the 1880s, but closed in 1923 when the castle's occupation by a military garrison ended. Although small, the layout, with two floors of cells built around an atrium, is similar to that of other contemporary prisons.

➠ *Exit right to the south battery.*

Dury's Battery   23

In 1708, after a French squadron was sighted in the Firth of Forth, it was decided to strengthen the castle's defences. The name of the battery commemorates its builder Captain Theodore Dury, who completed it in 1713. The iron guns on display are early 19th-century 18-pounders from the Napoleonic Wars.

➤ *Proceed northward, passing between, left, New Barracks (9) and the rear of Governor's House to the west edge of Castle Hill.*

Back Well **24**

The 'well', just 8 ft (2.5 m) deep, was excavated in 1628 to collect rainwater falling from the rock above.

➤ *Return southward, turn left and pass Governor's House. Enter the courtyard, left, between the sentry boxes.*

Ordnance Storehouse **25**

The courtyard was begun in 1747, when a gunpowder magazine was built at its west end. This was complemented five years later by storehouses to the north and south, which, in 1897, were converted to become the castle's military hospital, previously located in the Great Hall. At the west end, the magazine was demolished and replaced by stairs descending to the terrace, which had been built in 1858. Only from this point are there extensive views westward from Castle Rock.

When they were converted to jointly form the hospital, the north and south storehouses were given mock-medieval features, particularly the former, which was heightened. In 1997, the Scottish United Services Museum was transferred to the north block from Queen Anne Building in Crown Square and now occupies both buildings.

➤ *Return eastward to the Esplanade. Ahead lies the Royal Mile, which begins at the short thoroughfare called Castlehill.*

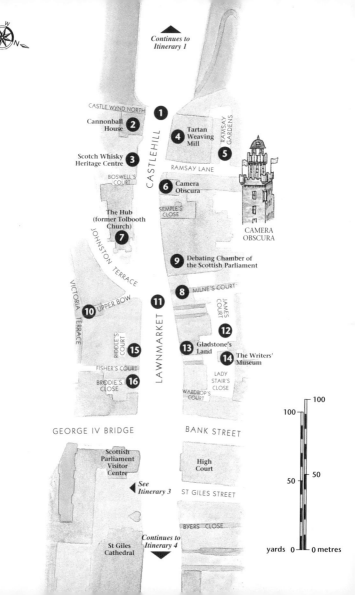

**Continues to
Itinerary 1**

CASTLE WYND NORTH

①

Cannonball
House ②

Tartan
Weaving
Mill ④

RAMSAY GARDENS

⑤

CASTLEHILL

Scotch Whisky
Heritage Centre ③

RAMSAY LANE

BOSWELL'S
COURT

Camera
Obscura ⑥

SEMPLE'S
CLOSE

CAMERA
OBSCURA

The Hub
(former Tolbooth
Church) ⑦

JOHNSTON TERRACE

Debating Chamber of
the Scottish Parliament ⑨

VICTORIA TERRACE

UPPER BOW

MILNE'S COURT ⑧

⑪

⑩

JAMES COURT

LAWNMARKET

⑫

RIDDLE'S
COURT

⑮

Gladstone's
Land ⑬

The Writers'
Museum ⑭

FISHER'S COURT

BRODIE'S
CLOSE ⑯

LADY
STAIR'S
CLOSE

WARDROP'S
COURT

GEORGE IV BRIDGE

BANK STREET

Scottish
Parliament
Visitor
Centre

High
Court

◄ **See
Itinerary 3**

ST GILES STREET

BYERS CLOSE

St Giles
Cathedral

**Continues to
Itinerary 4**
▼

100

100

50

50

yards 0

0 metres

The Royal Mile:
Castlehill and Lawnmarket

Scotch Whisky Heritage Centre –The Hub –
Gladstone's Land – Writers' Museum

These two streets mark the beginning of the Royal Mile, which runs eastward from Edinburgh Castle to the Palace of Holyroodhouse. Although short in length, this itinerary is packed with buildings and closes of historic interest; five museums are incorporated.

Timing: *Many will find it convenient to begin their exploration of the Royal Mile immediately following a morning visit to Edinburgh Castle. An obvious advantage of proceeding eastward from the castle is that the route is downhill. Wet weather need not deter the visitor, due to the number of buildings that can be entered.*

Location 1   Castlehill and the Royal Mile

Edinburgh's Old Town began to develop immediately outside the east gate of the castle when Castlehill's houses were built to accommodate members of the court. Subsequently, four more thoroughfares – Lawnmarket, High Street, Canongate and Abbey Strand – were laid out, virtually in a straight line as far as the Abbey of Holyrood, which lay 1940 yd – just over one mile – distant. In 1542, Edinburgh's royal residence was transferred from the castle to the Palace of Holyroodhouse, and the route between them soon became known as the Royal Mile; from the palace this route follows the ridge of the escarpment that rises gently westward towards its dramatic end at Castle Rock. For centuries, the Royal Mile, together with its subsidiary closes, *was* Edinburgh.

➠ *Proceed to the first building on the south side of Castlehill.*

Location 2   Cannonball House

356 Castlehill

Most of this building is relatively modern, but the wing that faces the castle dates from the 16th century. In the west wall of this, facing Castle Wynd, are embedded two cannonballs below the third-floor windows (the second is broken). These are alleged to have been fired from the castle during the 1754 siege; but some ascertain, less dramatically, that they were inserted to register the highest water level that could be reached by Edinburgh's first piped water supply in the mid-19th century.

On the pediment of a dormer window in the crowstepped south extension (best seen from the car park) are inscribed the initials of its first occupants, Alexander Muir and his wife, together with the date 1630.

➠ *Follow Castlehill eastward to the adjacent building.*

Location 3   Scotch Whisky Heritage Centre

354 Castlehill

❖ Open daily April to October 9.30am to 6.30pm, November to March 10am to 6pm. ❖ Admission charge.

Opened in 1993, the centre occupies the former Castlehill School, built in 1887 on the site of two ancient tenements. Visitors are shown how the distillation of Scotch whisky evolved, the highlight of the tour being a ride in a 'barrel', which trundles between tableaux. For an additional fee, a dram of blended whisky is offered to adults – but not before 12.30pm on Sundays. Brief lectures are given and a superficial video is shown. The full tour lasts around 50 minutes. Alternatively, a 15-minute barrel-ride-only version is available.

➠ *Cross to the north side of Castlehill.*

Location 4   Tartan Weaving Mill and Exhibition

555 Castlehill

❖ Open daily March to October, Monday to Saturday 9am to 6.30pm, Sunday 10am to 5pm; November to February, Monday to Saturday 9am to 5.30pm, Sunday 10am to 5pm. ❖ Admission charge to the exhibition.

Within the premises, the company operates a museum, shop, factory and restaurant. An exhibition covers every stage in the process of woollen cloth production: sheep shearing, carding the fibres, spinning, dyeing and finishing. Memories of tedious Industrial Revolution lectures at school will be aroused for many by examples of Hargreave's Spinning Jenny, Arkwright's Water-Powered Frame and Crompton's Mule – strangely unforgettable names. In the basement factory rather more modern machinery can be seen in operation. Highland dress from 1660 to the present is displayed. 'Be photographed in Highland Dress' and 'Try Weaving Yourself' are popular attractions.

Formerly, the building served as the Castle Hill Reservoir, having been built in

1850 on the site of Edinburgh's first reservoir, of 1720. Water was piped here from Comiston Springs, approximately 5 miles (8 km) south of the city. Originally, only five cisterns, all located along High Street, were supplied with the water.

➡ *Exit right to the west (castle) facing side of the building.*

Set in the wall, a fountain in Art Nouveau style commemorates the 300 citizens convicted of witchcraft and burned to death in Edinburgh 1479–1722. There is a descriptive plaque.

➡ *Return to Castlehill, left. First left Ramsay Lane. First left Ramsay Gardens.*

Location 5 Ramsay Gardens

Ramsay Gardens is a picturesque cul-de-sac created for Sir Patrick Geddes in 1894 to provide a hall of residence for students and a block of flats. It is said to be the world's first example of modern town planning. Incorporated in the scheme was Ramsay Lodge, a residence designed by Allan Ramsay, the poet, in 1740, and in which he and his son Allan Ramsay, the painter, both resided – little of this building is now visible.

➡ *Return to Castlehill and turn left.*

Location 6 Camera Obscura

Outlook Tower, 543-49 Castlehill

❖ Open April to October, Monday to Friday 9.30am to 6pm (later July and August), Saturday and Sunday 10am to 6pm (later during Festival); November to March 10am to 5pm. ❖ Admission charge.

Geddes purchased this tower in 1892 and fitted it out as 'the world's first socio-logical laboratory'. The four lower floors of the building, which were converted to tenements in the 17th century, are original, but the upper part of the building, with its exposed stonework, castellated roofline and short octagonal tower (of wood), was added in 1853 to accommodate Short's Observatory, operated by Maria Short, an optician. The original lens and mirror of her camera obscura, fitted at the top of the dome, were not replaced until 1945.

Panoramic views of the city are projected, every 20 to 30 minutes, onto a table (bright weather is essential for clarity), and a commentary is given. On the lower floors are displayed holograms, photographs of old Edinburgh and 'pinhole' photographs of the city taken with tins and cans serving as 'cameras'.

➡ *Exit left.*

The remainder of Castlehill's north side is formed by the rear of the Church of Scotland's General Assembly Hall, temporarily the debating chamber of the Scottish Parliament. This rather grim part of the complex was added in 1885 and extended in 1903.

➠ *Cross to the south side of Castlehill.*

Location 7 The Hub (former Tolbooth Church)

❖ Open daily 9.30am to 11pm (8am to 2am during the Festival). ❖ Admission free.

After conversion, this former church, disused since 1984, was opened in 1999 as The Hub, Edinburgh's Festival Centre. James Gillespie Graham and Augustus Pugin designed the building in Gothic Revival style, as the assembly hall and offices for the Church of Scotland. It was completed in 1844 and called The Victoria Hall.

The assembly relocated in 1929, and the building then served as a congregational church. Some services were held in Gaelic, and the church became known as the Highland Tolbooth St John's. Externally, the slender steeple, at 240 ft (73 m), even higher than the castle, is visible from many points in the city.

On the ground floor are shops and a restaurant. At the west end, the stairway is embellished with 200 plaster statuettes commissioned from Jill Watson. The stair leads to the former Assembly Hall, which has been splendidly restored, and incorporates Pugin's pulpit and screen. Various performances, mostly musical, take place within, many of them free. At other times visitors are welcome.

➠ *Exit from The Hub.*

The roundabout ahead marks the location of the Weigh House, where butter and cheese coming into the city were weighed. Around 1820, the structure had become redundant and was demolished to open up the road junction.

➠ *Cross to the north side of Castlehill.*

Location 8 Milne's Court

Milne's Court soon opens out to form a substantial courtyard. Immediately left (temporarily) is the public entrance to the Scottish Parliament. Robert Mylne (not Milne), Charles II's master mason, laid out the court in 1690 by demolishing small closes and building tenements to the north and south; in 1971 they were converted to halls of residence.

⟫ *Enter the Scottish Parliament's temporary Debating Chamber.*

Location 9   Temporary Debating Chamber of the Scottish Parliament

❖ Open Monday to Friday 9am to 12.30pm and 2pm to 4pm (closes at 4pm Friday). ❖ When in session, Parliament sits Wednesday afternoon and Thursday.

Public galleries accommodate up to 436 visitors, and the seats below 129 Members of the Scottish Parliament (MSPs). Unlike Westminster's House of Commons, each member is supplied with a microphone, and the semicircular layout of the seating is non-confrontational. The Presiding Officer, the equivalent to Westminster's Speaker, fronted by clerks, faces the members.

⟫ *Return to Castlehill and cross to Johnston Terrace immediately ahead. First left, Upper Bow, leads to Victoria Terrace.*

Location 10   Victoria Terrace

In the 1830s Victoria Terrace was created above Victoria Street's new shops (page 79). From here, views over the railings to the curving street below are exceptionally evocative of 'Old Edinburgh'. A plaque describes the complicated revision of West Bow's original layout when Victoria Street was built.

⟫ *Steps descend to Victoria Street, but a return northward to Lawnmarket should be made by those following this route. Cross to the north side of Lawnmarket, which begins at the Ensign Ewart pub.*

Location 11   Lawnmarket

This section of the Royal Mile formerly accommodated the agricultural produce market of Edinburgh; apparently, *lawn* meant 'inland' (as opposed to coastal), which is probably why the Lawnmarket was so-named. On Wednesdays, however, fabrics were sold, including linen, and as fine linen is still known as lawn it has been suggested that Lawnmarket's name may have referred to the linen market, but this seems less likely.

The Ensign Ewart, No. 521, one of the Royal Mile's smallest pubs, claims to have been established, at present basement level, in the 17th century.

⟫ *Continue eastward. First left James Court.*

Location 12   James Court

James Court was created in 1720, thirty years later than Milne's Court to its west, by removing closes in a similar way. It is much larger and has three entrances from Lawnmarket. The north block was built as tenements, but only its stone rubble east section is original, the rest being rebuilt in 1860 after a fire. Famous occupants include philosopher David Hume (1711–76) and James Boswell (1740–95). It was in his apartment in the court that Boswell entertained Dr Johnson on his arrival in Edinburgh in 1773.

➠ *Return by any south exit to Lawnmarket, left.*

Location 13   Gladstone's Land

477B Lawnmarket

❖ Open Monday to Saturday 10am to 4.30pm, Sunday (April to October only) 2pm to 4.30pm. ❖ Admission charge.

The house is believed to have been built around 1550, although there is some evidence that part of its fabric is earlier. A wealthy merchant, Thomas Gledstanes, purchased the building in 1617, and within three years had added a galleried front block overlooking Lawnmarket, which he refaced around 1621 with ashlar stonework. The house was then remodelled by Gledstanes as a tenement block, hence its name, *land* being old Scots for 'tenement'. In 1934, threatened with demolition, the building was presented to the National Trust for Scotland, which restored it. Further restoration in 1980 preceded the opening of the ground- and first-floor rooms to the public.

The facade of the five-storey-plus-attic building is little altered from the time of Gledstanes, although originally all the windows would have resembled those of the restored first and second floors. Arcaded shop fronts were once common in Edinburgh, but the double-arched example here is the only survivor of its type. Although external steps ascend directly to the first-floor stairs, visitors enter via the ground-floor shop.

Originally, the shop was leased by Gledstanes to a cloth seller, which is why cloth, manufactured and dyed in 17th-century style, is displayed. Nothing survives, however, of the shop's original interior.

➠ *From the end of the hall, stairs lead to the first floor, which was once let as a two-room flat. Pass through the little chamber to the middle room.*

Opposite: View of Victoria Street from Upper Bow

The existence of a large stone fireplace indicates that this was a kitchen. The bed recess in the wall is original.

Ahead, the Painted Chamber, Edinburgh's most compelling domestic interior, is part of Gledstane's front extension. Originally, its north (entrance) wall formed the external south wall of the house, the double doors gave access to a balcony, and to the west protruded an oriel window, as outlined by the existing recess. A deep, painted frieze on the entrance and east walls – an arcade with vases of flowers – was executed around 1620, but the simplified version on the west wall (above the fireplace) was added in 1980 for the sake of symmetry. Ceiling beams are decorated with a frieze of fruits, which is entirely original, although the colours have been somewhat 'muddied' by protective wax that was applied to them around 1934. The 17th-century four-poster bed was brought from Aberdeen.

The Green Room to the north-east, a later addition to the house, retains its original panelling, together with a built-in china cupboard and moulded stone chimneypiece. Dutch paintings include *Wooded Landscape with Peasants* by Jacob Ruisdael.

➽ *Return to the little chamber, from where modern stairs descend to the information room.*

More rooms with some 17th-century decoration, at present National Trust offices, exist up to fourth-floor level, but these are not open at present. Thomas Gledstanes is believed to have lived in a third-floor apartment, and the house remained in the possession of his family well into the 18th century.

➽ *Exit left. First left, Lady Stair's Close.*

A plaque above the archway to the close records that Robert Burns lodged in a house on its east side, a reference to his visit to Edinburgh in 1786, when he stayed in Baxters Close, which no longer exists.

➽ *Proceed ahead to the museum, left.*

Location 14   The Writers' Museum (Lady Stair's House)

Lady Stair's Close

❖ Open Monday to Saturday 10am to 5pm (Sunday 2pm to 5pm during the Festival). ❖ Admission free.

The name of the mansion commemorates Elizabeth, Dowager Countess of Stair, who purchased it in 1719. Very little of the original building, commissioned by merchant Sir Walter Gray in 1622, has survived.

By the late 19th century, the residence had become dilapidated and its north and south wings were demolished. The only external parts of the original house to survive are the lower two-thirds of its stair tower and, in the adjoining range, once the east wing, a central pediment flanked by two half pediments. The remainder is revival 17th-century Scots architecture, commissioned in 1897 by the 5th Earl of Rosebery, a descendant of Gray.

The original lintel above the entrance bears the initials WG and GS, of Sir William Gray and his wife Geida Smith, followed by 1622, the mansion's completion date.

Within, the interior is designed in mock-Jacobean style, but immediately right of the reception desk the moulded shafts and capitals of the chimneypiece are original. In 1907, shortly after its restoration, Lady Stair's House was returned to the city authorities by Lord Rosebery as a gift. It now accommodates the Writers' Museum, a tribute to three internationally renowned Scottish writers: Robert Louis Stevenson, Sir Walter Scott and Robert Burns, each of whom is allotted a floor.

The basement level is devoted to Robert Louis Stevenson, who was born in 1850, at 8 Howard Place, Edinburgh, a building that survives. Memorabilia include Stevenson's registration of birth, and many will be surprised to learn that the writer was baptised Robert, Lewis, Balfour, Stevenson. Much of his youth was spent in France, which is presumably why Lewis became Louis, but apparently he still sounded the 's'.

Exhibits feature a copy of *Young Folks* magazine, which incorporates the first instalment of *Treasure Island*; like the early works of Dickens, and the Sherlock Holmes stories of Conan Doyle, the book was originally published in instalments. Robert Louis Stevenson was never in robust health, and died on the island of Western Samoa in 1894, aged 44.

Exhibited in the ground-floor hall is the Walter Scott collection. This incorporates a great deal of memorabilia, including the writer's Meerschaum pipe, chess set and many original manuscripts; a reproduction of Scott's study includes items of his furniture. Sir Walter Scott was born in 1771 but he died in 1832 and was not, therefore, a Victorian, as many infer from his lengthy historical novels and his Victorian Gothic monument in Princes Street. Temporary exhibitions are held in the gallery above.

Steps ascend to the Burns room, where an audio presentation treats visitors to readings from Robert Burns in the authentic dialect. On display is the poet's writing desk, snuff box, portraits and manuscripts. Not a native of Edinburgh,

Robert Burns (1759–96), visited the city in November 1787 to promote sales of the Edinburgh edition of his *Poems chiefly in the Scottish Dialect*, which had been published in April that year. Although the words to the song 'Auld Lang Syne' are undoubtedly his best-known work, visitors who are unfamiliar with the poems of 'this heaven-taught plowman', will be astonished to discover how often they quote Burns (like Shakespeare) without realising it; some of his most famous lines are painted on the ceiling beams.

On the upper floor is displayed James Ballantyne's press, on which Walter Scott's *Waverley* novels were printed.

➥ *Exit and proceed eastward to the adjacent Wardrops Court.*

This court was created in the late 19th century by linking two small courts. At both entrances to the passageway from Lawnmarket are griffon (south side) and dragon (north side) brackets, fixed in 1892.

➥ *Exit right, Lawnmarket. Return to Gladstone's Land and cross to the south side of the road.*

Location 15   Riddle's Court

The names of Riddle's Close and Court commemorate Captain George Riddle, who rebuilt the Lawnmarket frontage in 1726. However, its prime interest is Bailie John McMorran's 16th-century mansion. McMorran, reputedly Edinburgh's wealthiest merchant, built two L-shaped blocks on the east, south and west sides of the court in 1590, probably occupying that on the south and west sides. Major alterations to the court were made in 1893, and restoration and partial conversion to an education centre took place in 1964.

Five years after building his mansion, McMorran was summoned to the High School to quell a riot by students objecting to a reduction in their holidays. Refusing to be threatened by a young student, William Sinclair, who was brandishing a pistol, McMorran bravely proceeded to enter the school and was shot dead. Sinclair escaped severe punishment due to the high position of his family, later becoming Sir William Sinclair of May.

In 1598 the Town Council held a banquet in McMorran's former house for James VI and his consort Queen Anne of Denmark. Philosopher David Hume lodged at Riddle's Court on his arrival in Edinburgh in 1751.

➥ *Return to Lawnmarket right. Second right Brodie's Close.*

Location 16   Brodie's Close

The name of this close commemorates Francis Brodie, a respected craftsman who lived here. His son William, a cabinet-maker, was even more highly respected, becoming Deacon of Wrights and Masons and a town councillor. Apparently, Brodie's day jobs were not sufficiently remunerative, for at night he indulged in armed burglary. During a failed raid on the Excise Office in Chessel's Court, Brodie was recognised, and a warrant for his arrest issued. Although he managed to escape to Holland, Brodie was extradited, tried, convicted and publicly hanged in Edinburgh, together with an accomplice, on 1 October 1788. It is said that the scaffold's trap-door mechanism had been designed by Brodie himself. Looking back towards Lawnmarket, the aspect of the close is one of the most picturesque in Edinburgh.

➠ *Return to Lawnmarket, right, and continue eastward. Cross to the Deacon Brodie pub on the north side of the road at the Bank Street junction ahead.*

The facade of the Deacon Brodie was built in 1894. Not only is it the largest hostelry on The Royal Mile, but also one of the most cheerful. As with many pubs in the city centre, drinks are likely to be served by a young Antipodean rather than a Scot!

Looking northward from Lawnmarket's corner with Bank Street, which was laid out in 1798 by the demolition of small closes, there is an excellent view of the Baroque 19th-century head office of the Bank of Scotland, which closes the vista. The bank (see page 76) is best admired at night, when it is floodlit.

Viewed eastward from the same corner, is the famous prospect of High Street, dominated by St Giles Cathedral (Itinerary 3), which is also floodlit at night.

The Royal Mile: St Giles Cathedral and the former Parliament House

This itinerary covers just a short section of the Royal Mile: the most westerly stretch of High Street. It is devoted to Edinburgh's High Kirk (generally known as St Giles Cathedral) and the buildings around the two squares in which it stands.

Timing: *The cathedral is open daily, but only after 1pm on Sunday. Parliament House may be viewed when the Law Courts are in session. Unfortunately, the general public are only permitted to view the Signet Library on Doors Open Day in September.*

Start: *The Bank Street/Lawnmarket junction. Remain on the north side of Lawnmarket.*

Fronting the north side of this, the last stretch of Lawnmarket, a coldly austere neo-Georgian pile, built in 1937 as the High Court of the Judiciary, is guaranteed to give anyone the shivers – even innocent defendants. Outside the entrance is a large bronze of philosopher David Hume (1711–76), cast in 1997.

Facing this, on the south side of the road, a brass 'I' set in the pavement marks the site of the gallows on which Deacon Brodie was hanged. The adjacent pyramidal well dates from 1835.

➧ *Continue eastward. First right West Parliament Square.*

Location 1   Scottish Parliament Committee Chambers

West Parliament Square

Providing the square's west range, right, this Grecian-style complex was built in 1818 as offices for the Midlothian County Council on a site formerly occupied by tenements. It is said that a sheriff had been impressed by a model of a temple on the Athens acropolis and asked the architect to copy it. Like the other buildings connected with the Scottish Parliament, it is expected that this will be vacated late in 2001. Entry to the Visitor Centre is from the west side (George IV Bridge).

The south side of the square primarily comprises the Signet Library, built by Robert Reid in 1812 (see page 44).

➧ *Proceed westward towards the large memorial.*

Location 2 Buccleuch Memorial

West Parliament Square

Even for the late-Victorian period, this memorial to the 5th Duke of Buccleuch (1806–84) is splendidly pompous. J. Edgar Boehm cast the bronze standing figure wearing Order of the Garter robes in 1888. Panels by various artists depict episodes in the duke's life, and his family's history; the battle scenes are particularly lively.

➠ *Continue ahead towards the railing adjacent to the north-west corner of St Giles.*

Location 3   The Heart of Midlothian

Set in the pavement, the heart-shaped arrangement of stones (setts) known as the Heart of Midlothian marks the entrance to the Old Tolbooth, which was built in the 14th century and stood until 1817. The name derives from the eponymous novel by Sir Walter Scott, in which he christened the Tolbooth, then a prison, the Heart of Midlothian. The building served in turn as the Scottish Parliament, a law court, an office for tax collection and, finally, a prison. By long tradition, to spit on the heart will bring good luck, and some Scotsmen still do so – no personal statement is being made against, for example, a tourist! Brass studs in the paving denote the area covered by the building, at the west end of which public hangings, including that of body-snatcher and murderer William Burke, took place on a first-floor balcony in 1829. William Hare, his accomplice, turned king's evidence and was reprieved.

➠ *Ahead, providing a splendid introduction to High Street, is St Giles Cathedral.*

Location 4   St Giles Cathedral (High Kirk of Scotland)

West Parliament Square

❖ Open (apart from services) Monday to Saturday 9am to 5pm (later in summer), Sunday 1pm to 5pm. ❖ Admission free.

Tower and spire

The tower and spire of St Giles are best appreciated from a short distance away to the south-west, or even better, south-east, of the church.

In spite of its late-medieval external appearance, only St Giles's tower and unusual spire, apart from a re-used doorway, predate William Burn's 19th-century refacing.

Around 1400, the lower stage of the tower had been completed, but the upper stage and crown spire were not built until the late 15th century. Each face of the tower is identical, but more important is the arched 'imperial' crown spire, constructed around 1474. Its design must have been considered particularly appropriate in view of Edinburgh's recently acquired status as royal capital. Much of the top section is mid-17th-century restoration work; however, the regilded weathercock dates from 1567. Recently restored are the festive, metal vanes supporting gold orbs, which had protruded from the pinnacles until their removal around 1800.

The Romanesque and the Gothic St Giles

There is evidence that St Giles, first recorded in 1178, was founded by Alexander I, who died in 1124. Apart from a fragment, nothing visible remains of this Romanesque church.

From the first, St Giles appears to have been a large building; it was completely rebuilt in the 14th century, and between the mid-15th and early 16th centuries, the period when the tower and spire were completed, private chapels were added, most of them on the south side, where the enormous churchyard of St Giles provided space for expansion. St Giles remained Edinburgh's only parish church until the Reformation.

Nineteenth-century refacing

By 1817, when both the Old and the New tolbooths, together with the lockenbooths (lock-up shops), had been removed, St Giles's newly-exposed walls were found to be in a terrible condition, and restoration was imperative. Between 1829 and 1833 William Burn completely refaced the body of the church in ashlar stone, reopening the west door and demolishing part of the nave's south aisle to give symmetry to the west front. He based his work on the English Decorated Gothic style (1290–1350) with its pinnacles and flamboyant tracery.

The portal of the west front, carved by John Rhind, was an 1884 replacement by William Hay, part of his modifications for Lord Provost Sir William Chambers. Burn's large window above the door survives.

Interior

Between the 16th and 19th centuries the interior was frequently remodelled to accommodate the changing needs of the Protestant church. In 1663 St Giles was designated a cathedral by Charles I and thus, for the first time, Edinburgh officially became a city. After the Civil War, even though the dean and bishop had been expelled, Edinburgh's High Kirk decided to remain accommodated in a 'cathedral' so that the city status would be retained. Although this is no longer necessary, the tradition has been maintained, and the building that technically should be known as the High Kirk of Edinburgh is still generally referred to as the Cathedral.

On occasions, St Giles accommodated up to four separate congregations in separate, partitioned areas, but since 1883 St Giles has been one unpartitioned church.

As part of the Chambers remodelling of 1871–83, designed to make St Giles the 'Westminster Abbey' of Scotland, the church was provided with a new set of furnishings, which would be followed by a proliferation of monuments.

The screen within the entrance was made of reused woodwork from Queen Victoria's pew; carved on its east side are VR and the royal arms.

Nave

In 1871, William Hay began alterations for Sir William Chambers by removing the first of the building's internal partitions. His work ended in 1883 with the nave, where he replaced Burn's recently erected arcades to the aisles.

The medieval roof is believed to have been of timber; surprisingly, its 14th-century stone replacement lasted until Burn created the present vault of plaster.

The nave's upper windows (clerestory) on both sides are another addition by Burn, who designed them to match the 15th-century examples in the chancel. Above the arches of the south arcade are outlines of the medieval clerestory, but the north wall had none.

In front of the north arcade's third pier from the west stands a life-size bronze statue of John Knox, by Pittendrigh MacGillivray, 1905. Knox, Minister of St Giles 1560–72, was first buried in the graveyard of St Giles; however, the precise location of his remains is unknown.

Above the crossing's arch are indications of the chancel's former roof level.

➡ *Proceed clockwise around the building.*

Albany Aisle

The west end of the North Aisle retains its medieval rib vault, which also covers the two-bay Albany Aisle in the north-west corner. The capital of the aisle's central column is carved and painted on its north and south faces respectively with the arms of Robert, Duke of Albany (died 1420) and Archibald, 4th Earl of Douglas (died 1424). Both were accused of implication in the murder, in 1402, of David, Duke of Rothesay, son of Robert III and heir to the throne. It has been suggested that they may have financed the building of the aisle in expiation of the crime.

Scots who fell in both World Wars are also commemorated in the aisle.

A brass, low on the north transept's wall, marks the former position of a doorway from which stairs led to the priest's room where Sir John Gordon of Haddo was imprisoned in 1644. The room became known as Haddo's Hole; it later served as a Covenanters' prison, but was demolished around 1790.

St Eloi Aisle

The archway opening onto the next aisle matches the height of the lost medieval arcades of the nave's aisles, with which it is contemporary. Set in the aisle's west wall is a Romanesque scallop capital, discovered in 1880. Although not in situ, this is the only visible feature that is known to have come from the 12th-century St Giles. The large Jacobean Revival monument against the north wall to Archibald, Marquess of Argyll (1598–1661) was made in 1895; the recumbent figure of the marquess, a Covenanting leader beheaded at the Mercat Cross outside St Giles in 1661, is by Charles McBride. A crowned hammer depicted in the centre of the mosaic floor and on the vault above the window, commemorates the aisle's foundation around 1410 by the Hammermen, Edinburgh's leading medieval trades guild. Stained glass in the window illustrates the arms of leading Covenanters.

Looking back from the centre of the nave, a good view of the west window may be gained. In 1985 its Victorian stained glass was replaced with the present tribute to poet Robert Burns by the Icelander Leifur Breidfjord.

Crossing

The crossing retains its medieval vault, and the four octagonal piers appear to date from the early 15th century, but might be earlier.

St Giles Cathedral

North Transept

This is roofed by another of Burn's plaster vaults, but the arches between it and the crossing are basically original. The north bay, now fitted as a vestibule, is separated by a stone screen designed by Hay. Figures commemorate members of Edinburgh's former trade guilds and their patron saints.

Chambers Aisle

Immediately east of the north vestibule, this aisle was created from the former vestry in 1891 to honour Lord Provost Sir William Chambers (1800–83). Its west window, left, is a late 14th-century survivor from the former St John's Chapel, which Burn's vestibule replaced. Also late 14th century are two brackets designed respectively as a lion's head and a rosette; these were found above the window and reset in the arch. The 14th-century rib vault incorporates a medieval central boss found outside the church when the aisle was under construction.

Chancel

Although heavily restored by Hay, St Giles's chancel is still reputedly the finest example of late Gothic work to survive in a Scottish parish church. Originally, the medieval chancel and its aisles, begun around 1400, were the same height, but almost fifty years later partial rebuilding, including the addition of a clerestory, necessitated a new, higher roof vault. This is probably why it was decided to raise the height of the tower, which would otherwise have looked squat.

➠ *Pass the ironwork screen.*

It is noticeable that the piers of the two most easterly bays, which were rebuilt around 1453, are more profusely carved and their windows deeper: alterations connected with the application for St Giles to be given collegiate status, which was granted in 1467. Rediscovered in 1871 was the 15th-century tomb recess in the penultimate bay.

From the centre of the church, looking westward, may be seen the panel above the chancel arch painted with the Arms of George II in 1736. This originally formed the back of the royal pew, which had been located in the first-floor gallery but was resited during the Chambers remodelling.

➠ *Cross to the large chapel in the south-east corner.*

Thistle Chapel (donations by visitors are requested)

Robert Lorimer completed this large chapel for the Order of the Thistle in 1911. Money was donated to the Order in 1905 for restoring its chapel at Holyrood Abbey (a revival of James VII's plan), but this proved impracticable, and work began on the present site within St Giles in 1909.

➡ *The chapel is entered via its ante-chapel.*

The quality of the woodwork carved by the Clow brothers is exceptionally high, in particular the knights' stalls, with their pointed canopies surmounted by crested helmets, and their arms painted on the backs; the larger stall is that of the sovereign. The Communion Table commemorates George V, and a gilded floor slab his son George VI.

Preston Aisle

In the mid-15th century, the church was presented with an arm-bone relic of St Giles by Sir William Preston, and in gratitude the Town Council commissioned the three-bay Preston Aisle. Preston's arms are carved on a boss dating from around 1487. Reset in the wall immediately left, beside the permanently closed gate to the Thistle Chapel, a medieval carving of an angel bears Edinburgh's arms. Beneath this, a stone tablet commemorates R.S. Lorimer (1864–1929), architect of the Thistle Chapel. Inscribed fragments of medieval burial stones are incorporated in the wall below.

Chepman Aisle

An archway from the Preston Aisle's west bay, its top part formerly a window, frames the Chepman Aisle. Consecrated in 1513, the aisle commemorates Walter Chepman, Scotland's first printer, who founded the chapel. Chepman's arms impaling those of his first wife are carved on the roof boss. Originally, this chapel was dedicated to St John the Evangelist, whose eagle emblem is carved on the central bracket of the west wall. Against the east wall stands a polychrome 1889 monument, in Jacobean style, to James Graham, Marquess of Montrose (1612–50), who was hanged at the Mercat Cross.

Near the entrance to the aisle is displayed one of the four original copies of the National Covenant, signed in 1638.

On the floor, facing the pulpit, against a south aisle pier, the Vesper Bell is the only medieval example in the church to have survived; it bears an inscription and the date 1504.

Further west, a floor bronze marks where, in 1637, Jenny Geddes is reputed to have thrown her stool at Dean Hannay in protest against the new litany introduced by Charles I.

Moray Aisle/Holy Blood Aisle

The name of the three-bay Moray Aisle, created in 1830, commemorates Regent Moray, half-brother of Mary, Queen of Scots.

Opening from the east end of the Moray Aisle, the Holy Blood Aisle was founded by Edinburgh merchants as the Holy Blood Chapel in 1518. Although small, it retains the most elaborate Gothic feature of St Giles: a sumptuously decorated recess, the purpose of which is uncertain. Windows in the aisle depict the assassination of Regent Moray in 1569.

A monument to Regent Moray, made shortly after his death, was destroyed in the late 18th century, but its brass plate survived and has been incorporated in the present Renaissance-style monument of 1864, which is based on a contemporary illustration of the original.

A plaque towards the west end of the south wall is simply inscribed: 'Thank God for James Young Simpson's discovery of chloroform anaesthesia in 1847.'

A life-size bronze of 1904 against the west wall of the Moray Aisle commemorates the Edinburgh-born writer Robert Louis Stevenson (1850–94).

➠ *Exit left from St Giles left to West Parliament Square.*

The New Tolbooth was built outside the south-west corner of St Giles in 1561, hiding much of it. This was demolished in 1807, but more than twenty years would pass before Burn began his restoration work on the church at this point. After he had removed the south bay of the former west front for reasons of symmetry, Burn replaced it with an entrance, approached by steps, to the Moray Aisle. Its oriel window incorporates cusped windows and a bracket carved with an angel bearing a shield, replicas of similar devices on the medieval oriel above the south porch, which Burn initially had intended to preserve.

➠ *The entrance to the Signet Library is located at the east end of West Parliament Square's south facade.*

Location 5 Signet Library

West Parliament Square

❖ Open 'Doors Open Day' in September, 10am to 5pm. ❖ Admission charge.

Although Robert Reid built the shell of the library 1809–12, it is the interior work by William Stark that is exceptional. Unfortunately, Stark died in 1813, and William Playfair completed his scheme. Stark brilliantly overcame the restrictions of the long, narrow plan by creating nave/aisle layouts, screens and a series of flattened domes.

At first-floor level, a Corinthian screen designed by Playfair in 1820 fronts a glass-domed vestibule. Within the Upper Library, originally built for the Faculty of Advocates, Stark excelled himself to such a degree that George IV described it as the most beautiful room he had ever seen. The Corinthian capitals were carved by John Steell, and the central, shallow glass dome was painted with an Apollo and the Muses theme by Thomas Stothard. Originally, the delicately balustraded gallery ran around all four walls, but its west section was removed in 1889, when the stained-glass window commemorating Queen Victoria's Diamond Jubilee was inserted.

➠ *Exit right to Parliament Square.*

Location 6   Parliament Square

Reid adopted some unused designs by Robert Adam to provide a palatial unifying frontage to the square, which comprised the 17th-century Parliament House in its south-west corner and a variety of 19th-century legal buildings, most of which Reid had built earlier. His work proceeded in two stages; the first, 1804-06, included the Signet Library and Parliament House; the second, 1827-38, extended his scheme eastward, a fire in 1824 having destroyed existing buildings on the east side of the square, which had to be rebuilt completely.

A rusticated arcade, Ionic loggias and a rooftop balustrade give strength and delicacy to much of the facade. Unfortunately, this is not matched by its centrepiece, which comprises an undecorated pediment supported by enormous but unfluted Ionic columns, resulting in a ponderous appearance. On the east side of the square, Reid repeated his elevations on the west side, thereby achieving a 'mirror image' symmetry.

➠ *To visit Parliament House, proceed to the entrance to the lobby in the south-west quadrant.*

Location 7   Parliament House

11 Parliament Square

❖ Open when courts are in session: Monday to Friday 10am to 1pm and 2pm to 4pm. ❖ Admission free.

When James V established the judicial supremacy of the new Court of Session in 1532, its accommodation was shared with the Scottish Parliament, which then sat only occasionally, and in brief sessions. Cramped accommodation in the Old Tolbooth was all that Edinburgh offered Parliament until 1560, when the three west bays of St Giles were partitioned off as an annexe. However, in 1632 Charles I commissioned the present Parliament House, and the Scottish Parliament sat here from 1639 until 1707, when its members transferred to Westminster following the Act of Union.

The hall was ready for occupation by 1639, its hammerbeam roof of Danish oak, an extremely late Gothic example, having been made by John Scott, who used no nails in its construction. The stone brackets are carved with beasts, portraits and depictions of castles.

➠ *Enter the hall from its east doorway and turn right.*

Apart from the roof, most internal features are 19th-century, all the window tracery dating from 1870, when a great deal of remodelling took place.

Two statues by Chantrey stand against the north wall: Viscount Melville, carved in 1818, and Robert Dundas, carved in 1824.

Against the east wall, the finest statue in the hall, of a dramatically gesticulating Judge Duncan Forbes, 1852, is by the great French sculptor Roubiliac.

Stained glass depicting the founding of the Court of Sessions was made at Munich in 1868 for the large south window. Originally an embellishment to the main entrance of Parliament House, the figures of Justice and Mercy, made by Alexander Mylne in 1637, have been restored and stand outside the south door.

The figure of Sir Walter Scott, in a west wall niche, was carved by John Greenshields in 1830, two years after the writer had modelled for it; the plinth is inscribed 'Sic Sedebat' (Thus he used to sit). Scott served as a principal clerk of the sessions, 1806–30.

The Lords Ordinary last sat in the hall in 1844, and Parliament House is now a venue in which counsel and solicitors confer informally.

➠ *Exit from Parliament House, right.*

Location 8   Charles II Statue

Parliament Square

Cast in lead, probably in Holland, Charles II is depicted life-size as a Roman emperor on horseback. The statue was erected here in 1685, but has been restored several times and moved slightly eastward. It is a replica of a Grinling Gibbons bronze statue at Windsor, made in 1680. The pedestal's marble tablet, inscribed in Latin, is original, but the pedestal itself is a 19th-century copy of Robert Mylne's work of 1685.

➠ *Exit right and proceed towards the east end of St Giles.*

At the south-east corner of the church, impressive steps lead directly to the

Thistle Chapel's ante-chapel; these were originally intended for use by members of the Order of the Thistle for their installation services, but are now used by the public for access to church services. The 15th-century doorway comes from the nave's former south porch. At the east end of the chancel, Burn made few alterations apart from introducing buttresses.

➠ *Proceed to the Mercat Cross, at the north-east corner of St Giles.*

Location 9   Mercat Cross

Parliament Square

Beside the Mercat Cross, which was first recorded in 1365 and primarily served as a drinking water fountain, royal proclamations preceded by a fanfare of trumpets were made by Lord Lyon, King of Arms. Members of the nobility who had been sentenced to death were executed here in public, and it was also a favoured meeting place for merchants, who continued to negotiate at the cross after a covered exchange had been built for them at City Chambers, opposite.

It is known that the cross has occupied at least five sites in High Street. A version of 1617 was removed in 1756, and it was not until 1866 that a replacement was erected. However, Prime Minister Gladstone appears to have found this inadequate, and personally donated money for the present structure, which was designed by Sydney Mitchell and completed in 1885. Every version appears to have followed the same basic design of a deep, octagonal base from which rises a shaft surmounted by a unicorn. Dragons cavort amid foliage on the shaft's early 15th-century capital, the only medieval feature of the cross to survive; the shaft itself is a 1970 replacement and the unicorn dates from 1869. Supported by a platform, the base, decorated with painted and gilded arms, is somewhat smaller than its predecessors; the carved arms of Edinburgh on the south face were copied from a panel of the 1617 cross. Above the wooden door in the base, the Latin inscription, composed by Gladstone, is dated 24 November 1885.

➠ *Continue anticlockwise around St Giles.*

Between the second and third buttresses of the chancel's north aisle, a 17th-century panel bears the crest of the Napier family.

Like its counterpart on the south side, the north transept is flanked by low, late 19th-century extensions.

➠ *To continue with Itinerary 4, cross to the north side of High Street and proceed to Advocates' Close.*

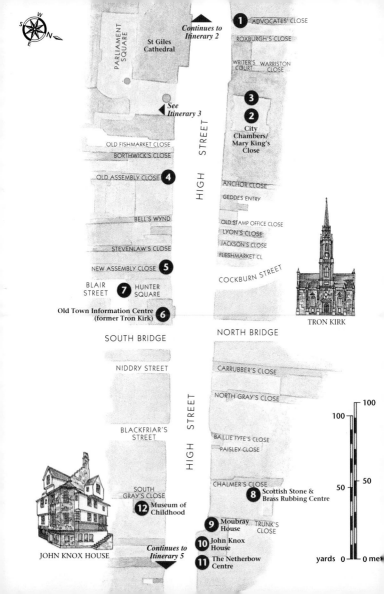

W N E S

PARLIAMENT SQUARE

St Giles Cathedral

1 ADVOCATES' CLOSE

ROXBURGH'S CLOSE

WRITER'S WARRISTON
COURT CLOSE

*Continues to
Itinerary 2*

*See
Itinerary 3*

3

2
City
Chambers/
Mary King's
Close

ANCHOR CLOSE

GEDDES ENTRY

OLD STAMP OFFICE CLOSE

LYON'S CLOSE

JACKSON'S CLOSE

FLESHMARKET CL

HIGH STREET

OLD FISHMARKET CLOSE

BORTHWICK'S CLOSE

OLD ASSEMBLY CLOSE **4**

BELL'S WYND

STEVENLAW'S CLOSE

NEW ASSEMBLY CLOSE **5**

BLAIR
STREET

7 HUNTER
SQUARE

Old Town Information Centre
(former Tron Kirk) **6**

COCKBURN STREET

TRON KIRK

SOUTH BRIDGE

NORTH BRIDGE

NIDDRY STREET

CARRUBBER'S CLOSE

NORTH GRAY'S CLOSE

BLACKFRIAR'S
STREET

HIGH STREET

BAILLIE FYFE'S CLOSE

PAISLEY CLOSE

CHALMER'S CLOSE

SOUTH
GRAY'S CLOSE

8 Scottish Stone &
Brass Rubbing Centre

12 Museum of
Childhood

9 Moubray
House

TRUNK'S
CLOSE

JOHN KNOX HOUSE

*Continues to
Itinerary 5*

10 John Knox
House

11 The Netherbow
Centre

100

100

50

50

yards 0

0 me

The Royal Mile: High Street

Mary King's Close – Scottish Stone and Brass Rubbing Centre –
John Knox House – Museum of Childhood

Much of the charm of this itinerary is due to the remarkable number of ancient, narrow closes that punctuate both sides of High Street. The former Trinity College Church, which now accommodates the Scottish Stone and Brass Rubbing Centre, is a rare Edinburgh example of a medieval ecclesiastical building.

Timing: *Bookings must be made in advance to visit the subterranean Mary King's Close. Six other buildings may also be entered, but dry weather for the tour is preferable.*

Start: *Advocates' Close, on the north side of High Street, faces the nave of St Giles and links with Itinerary 3.*

Location 1 Advocates' Close

A wall plaque at the High Street end of the approach to Advocates' Close commemorates former residents Lord Advocate Sir James Stewart (1692–1713), Andrew Crosbie, 'the jovial counsellor Pleydell' and the 19th-century Court painter Sir John Scougal. The door lintels on the building opposite bear inscriptions dated 1590.

No. 8, DOM, an art shop, may be Edinburgh's oldest house; a date of 1475 has been suggested. Visitors are welcome to explore.

➠ *Return to High Street, left.*

Location 2 City Chambers

High Street

❖ The Old Council Chamber may be viewed when not in use.

City of Edinburgh Council still convenes at City Chambers, The Royal Mile's only public building to predate the 19th century. The site chosen for it had been occupied by the Provost of Edinburgh's mansion in which Mary, Queen of Scots spent her last night in the city, 15 June 1567. John Adam's design was accepted in 1753, but several amendments were made as work progressed.

Originally, it was planned that City Chambers would house various council meeting halls, a library, a Register House, the official residence of the Lord Provost and covered accommodation for a Merchants' Exchange. However, when City Chambers was finished, in 1761, only one public office was accommodated, the remainder being leased for a variety of uses. It was not until 1893 that the local authority gained sole possession – 132 years later than planned!

A shopping arcade, an afterthought, which served to screen the building from the street, was replaced in 1901 by the present much narrower arcade, the central arches of which now shelter a World War I and II monument, designed by Sir Edwin Lutyens in 1927. Wings were added with sensitivity to the building in 1934. Dominating the courtyard, the bronze of Alexander the Great training his horse Bucephalus, was modelled by John Steell in 1832, cast in 1883 and transferred here from St Andrew Square in 1916.

➥ *To view the Old Council Chamber enter the building and proceed to reception.*

Internally, the first-floor Old Council Chamber, initially leased to the government as a Customs House, has been little altered. Council meetings were held in the chamber for the first time in 1811. At the entrance, the Corinthian screen is original, but the panelling dates from 1903.

➥ *Exit from City Chambers and cross to Parliament Square for the tour of Mary King's Close, which must be booked in advance and commences beside the Mercat Cross.*

Location 3   Mary King's Close

City Chambers

❖ Daily tours at intervals 10.30am to 9.30 pm, organised by Mercat Tours, tel: 0131 225-2591. ❖ Admission charge.

Now completely covered over and eerily evoking a Scottish Pompeii, Mary King's Close was laid out in the 16th century to wind downhill from High Street towards the Nor'Loch. Its name is said to record a well-known publican, whose tavern stood in the close. Here also lived Andrew Bell, later to found *Encyclopaedia Britannica*. The entire close remained open to the sky until the mid-18th century, when most of it was utilised to provide part of the foundations of City Chambers. Virtually unknown to visitors until comparatively recently, the hidden close was featured in a Billy Connolly television series, and is now a major tourist attraction.

Mary King's Close is not unique in Edinburgh, as much of the Old Town is built over several storeys of earlier buildings; it is, however, the most accessible. Edinburgh was hit by plague in 1645, and the inhabitants of Mary King's Close, where many died, are said to have been the last to become infected. Even when the epidemic appeared to have ended, all its properties were sealed for fear that some trace might survive within them and break out. Eventually, brave occupants returned to live in the houses, in spite of the tales of ghostly apparitions then current.

Many residents from houses at the south end objected to being evicted from them when the construction of City Chambers began over the close in 1753, and the first compulsory purchase order in Scotland had to be invoked. The north end of the close survived until 1856, when Cockburn Street was cut through it to provide better access from the Old Town to Waverley Station. Even after this, however, some properties were doggedly occupied until the end of the 19th century.

Visitors are conducted to Mary King's Close, which begins at the south-west corner of City Chambers, from where it runs parallel with Warriston Close, located high above and slightly to the west. In view of its history and long abandonment, most visitors are surprised to discover how much of this ancient cobbled wynd has survived. Much of the wall fabric of the houses, with spaces for windows and doorways, may still be seen, but not, of course, their roofs; some rooms even retain fireplaces and shelving. A baker's shop can be identified, and the ceiling hooks in another house are possibly those from which Mr Chesney, a sawmaker, suspended his blades until forced to vacate the premises in 1896.

➤ *Return to High Street, left. First left Anchor Close.*

The name of Anchor Close commemorates the Anchor Tavern, which once stood here. Robert Burns is believed to have visited the hostelry in the company of William Smellie, whose printing press stood nearby. On it was produced the first edition of *Encyclopaedia Britannica* in 1768 and the Edinburgh edition of Burns's poems in 1787. Burns recorded in verse that Smellie had a caustic wit but a benevolent heart.

➤ *Cross to the south side of High Street and return westward to where Old Fishmarket Close faces the east wing of City Chambers.*

Stones set in a polygonal shape in the pavement west of the entrance to the close mark one of the five locations of the Mercat Cross.

➤ *Return eastward. First right Borthwick's Close.*

The Cross Well of 1785, with its unusual stepped top, marks the narrow (less than 6 ft or 2 m) entrance to Borthwick's Close.

Located at 180 High Street are the headquarters of the Festival Fringe Society.

➤ *Continue eastward. First right Old Assembly Close.*

Location 4   Old Assembly Close

On the pavement, at the entrance to the close, the High Street Wellhead was
founded around 1675. An assembly hall that stood here until the 18th century is
commemorated by the name of this close. On the west side, right, the Jacobean-
style detailing of George Heriot's School, built in 1840, pays homage to the original foundation, near Greyfriars Church (page 88). It was in a tenement at the
High Street end of this close that a devastating fire broke out on the night of 15
November 1824; during the conflagration, most of the south side of High Street
from Parliament Square to the Tron Kirk was destroyed.

➤ *Exit right. Fourth right New Assembly Close.*

Location 5   New Assembly Close

A pedimented archway provides a suitably classical entrance to this close, which is
dominated by a Grecian-style villa built for the Commercial Bank by James
Gillespie Graham in 1814 (now the Lord Reid Building).

The name of the close commemorates the New Assembly Rooms, 1776–84,
which took over the function of the building in Old Assembly Close. It was
accommodated in the early 18th-century building (not visible) that survives to
the rear of the Lord Reid Building. Formal ballroom dances were an extremely
fashionable pursuit at the time, and appear to have been the most popular functions held in the rooms.

➤ *Continue eastward and cross to the south side of High Street to view the north facade
of the former Tron Kirk.*

Location 6   Old Town Information Centre

Tron Kirk, High Street

❖ Open April to September, Monday to Saturday 10am to 5pm.

When St Giles was given cathedral status in 1633, it was no longer permitted to
function as the parish church of Edinburgh, and the Tron Kirk was constructed
1636–47 to accommodate its congregation. The name reflects that to the north
stood the Salt Tron (beam) from which the weight of salt brought into the city
could be measured.

John Mylne junior designed the building in the English Renaissance style of the
period, but also incorporated some Dutch features, in particular the central door,
which is surmounted by an inscribed cartouche and flanked by Ionic pilasters

supported by panelling. In 1785, the church had to be foreshortened for the creation of South Bridge and Hunter Square, which resulted in the present barn-like body of the building. The half bays left at each end were then given their pairs of Ionic pilasters.

After the fire of 1824, the tower had to be demolished but it was soon rebuilt – much higher than before, and surmounted by a spire.

➤ *Cross to Hunter Square, which runs behind the church.*

The south facade of the church retains fewer original features, as its aisle was demolished in 1787. In recompense, the facade was given a pediment and mid-17th-century-style tracery added to the blocked windows.

➤ *Enter the building from the north door.*

The Tron Kirk was closed for worship in 1952, but now houses the Old Town Information Centre. Nothing survives of the gallery that ran across three walls, and all the fittings have been removed. The original porch at the tower's base does remain, however, as do the stairs that formerly led to the galleries. Retained is the hammerbeam roof which, as at Parliament Hall, was built by John Scott, and is equally impressive.

Exhibitions arranged by the Old Town Information Centre deal with Edinburgh's history, and supplement the displays in the Huntly House Museum. At the lower level may be seen the excavated Marlyn's Wynd, a cobbled close laid out in 1532 between High Street and Cowgate. Its paving stones are original and believed to be the oldest in the city.

➤ *Exit and return southward to Hunter Square.*

Location 7   Hunter Square

This attractive square, laid out to the south of the Tron Kirk, is linked with South Bridge to the east and Blair Street to the south; together they formed one of Edinburgh's most important late 18th-century developments. Fortunately, much of Robert Kay's classical architecture to the south and west sides of the square has survived, his south block being the least altered.

Hunter Square has become a popular gathering place during the Edinburgh Festival, when street entertainers take over. At other times it currently finds favour as a rendezvous for alfresco drinkers.

➤ *Exit from the west side of the square to South Bridge, left. First right High Street. Cross to the north side and continue eastward to the entrance, sixth left, to Paisley's Close (Nos 97–103 High Street).*

Beneath the oriel window above the entrance arch to the close a portrait head of a youth, carved by John Rhind, is surmounted by the inscription 'Heave awa chaps, I'm no dead yet'. These brave words were uttered to his rescuers by twelve-year-old Joseph McIver, who was buried under rubble following the collapse, in 1861, of the tenement building in which he had lived. Although the lad survived without serious injury, thirty-five residents lost their lives in the disaster; surprisingly, the six-storey rear wing of the tenement, built around 1700, has survived.

➧ *Continue eastward. First left Chalmers Close. Descend the steps.*

Location 8   Scottish Stone and Brass Rubbing Centre (former Trinity College Church)

Chalmers Close

❖ Open April to September, Monday to Saturday 10am to 5pm (Sundays during the Festival 2pm to 5pm). ❖ Admission free; a charge is levied for making rubbings.

Trinity College, a monastic establishment, was founded in the valley between the Old Town and Calton Hill by Mary of Gueldres, consort of James II, in the mid-15th century. Work on the aisled chancel of its church began around 1460 and continued until the end of the century. Transepts, a crossing and a stubby, pitch-roofed tower were added around 1530, but the projected nave was not built.

At the Reformation, the church served the local parish from around 1580 to 1848, when the site was acquired for the construction of Waverley Station. Fortunately, the building was dismantled rather than demolished, each stone being numbered before being put into store. In 1872 the body of the chancel was rebuilt on the present site, but not its aisles or the transepts and tower of the church, too many of the stones having disappeared, presumably stolen by builders. Ironically, the church at last received a nave, which protruded from the centre of the chancel's north wall; thankfully, this pointless addition was removed in 1964.

Facing Chalmers Close, the west wall now incorporates the Perpendicular window that formerly lit one of the transepts; its loop tracery is typical of the 1530s. Two carved shields above the window, formerly capitals, bear respectively the initials IB and ID of two 16th-century provosts of the college: John Brady and John Dingwall.

The south wall's three clerestory windows remain *in situ*, but the lower windows came from the walls of the lost south aisle; however, none of the tracery is original. A few stones around the windows retain the key numbers that were painted on them to aid reconstruction when they were dismantled in 1848.

The north wall was reconstructed minus its windows as it had been decided that this was where the nave would join the chancel. The point of juncture is now indicated by rendering. The apse is seen later.

➠ *Enter the building.*

The lofty rib vault of this relatively small building immediately impresses in a regal manner as befits a royal church. On the south wall can be seen the outline of the aisle arcade, now filled. Inset in this wall is the original piscina (hand basin) of the vestry. Fitted in the west wall is an outstanding 15th-century fireplace from a demolished house that stood nearby. The 'Trinity Panels', painted for the church probably by the Flemish master Hugo van der Goes (c.1440–82), have survived and may be seen in the National Gallery of Scotland (page 109).

Carved stones and brasses from all parts of Scotland are now displayed within the building, and rubbings may be made.

➠ *Return to High Street, left. First left Trunk's Close.*

Only from Trunk's Close can the apse of Trinity College Church be seen. Although its tall lancet windows have lost their tracery they remain imposing. Set above them are sections of capitals from other parts of the church.

On the east side of the close can be seen what now forms the rear wing of Moubray House but was possibly the original building.

➠ *Return to High Street, left.*

The stone Fountain Well on the broad pavement in front of Moubray House was erected in 1813.

Location 9   Moubray House

51-53 High Street

The development, general layout and internal decoration of this house, one of Edinburgh's most ancient, has much in common with Gladstone's Land in Lawnmarket. Built of stone rubble, the High Street frontage was constructed around 1630; it now incorporates a timber-framed attic floor, a 19th-century doorway approached by steps and a modern shop front.

The name of the house commemorates Andrew Moubray, who built a tenement here in 1529, which may have been the existing wing to the rear. An extension towards High Street was built later in the 16th century, and it is presumed that, as at Gladstone's Land, this would have been fronted with protruding wooden galleries, which marked the point where the present stone rubble facade was eventually constructed.

From his office within, Daniel Defoe, author of *Robinson Crusoe,* edited the *Edinburgh Courant* in 1710. Later in the century Moubray House became a tavern, but in 1890 its new owner 'took the pledge' and the building was converted to a temperance hotel.

Adjoining Moubray House to the east is an even more picturesque contemporary building.

Location 10 John Knox House

45 High Street

❖ Open Monday to Saturday, 10am to 5pm (last entry 4.30pm). ❖ Admission charge.

There is no evidence for the long-established tradition that the Protestant reformer John Knox (1505–72) ever lived here. Nevertheless, it has ensured the continued existence of this ancient dwelling, externally the most picturesque in Edinburgh. In 1849 many wanted to demolish the house in order to widen the High Street, and following this narrow escape the Church of Scotland purchased and restored the building, which was opened as a museum in 1853; further restoration took place in 1958.

Apart from the Georgian sash windows and early-Victorian external stairs, the exterior of the building dates from the 16th century; its medieval (probably late 15th-century) predecessor, the original house, was only two storeys high and stood further back. More storeys and an extension towards the street were added either when John Arres inherited the house in 1525, or following damage caused during the English sack of Edinburgh in 1544.

Carved below the first-floor windows that overlook High Street are a garlanded coat of arms and IM and MA, the initials of goldsmith James Mossman and his wife Mariotta Arres, who inherited the house in 1556. Mary, Queen of Scots appointed Mossman Assaye of the Mint; a firm supporter of the queen, he was executed for treason in 1573.

Above the doorway and windows of the shop front runs a 16th-century inscription, which, in modern English, reads 'Love God above all, and your neighbour as yourself'. On the corner, at first-floor level, a sundial is set below a carving of

Opposite: John Knox House

Moses pointing to the sun appearing from behind a cloud inscribed 'God' in Greek, Latin and English.

The house is entered from the shop door. In front of the south windows stands a miniature pulpit, which formerly was fixed outside the house around the carved figure of Moses. Displays within the museum detail the lives of Knox and James Mossman – 'the preacher and the goldsmith'.

Both upper floors comprise two main rooms. In the first-floor front room a fireplace retains its Dutch flowervase-pattern tiles.

The second floor's front room, part of the extension, is the most interesting in the house. Its beamed ceiling, with early 17th-century decoration, is original; the painted Cain and Abel panel of around 1640 and the Renaissance-style arcaded panelling were probably brought from elsewhere. A seemingly haphazard combination of venerable Dutch and Flemish tiles surrounds the fireplace. Also, overlooking the street is a small gallery with a fireplace around which tiles depict the Last Supper. Above this, carved on the panelling, are a lion and the date 31 October AD 1561.

In the rear room, a priest and two crucifixion scenes are depicted in the Flemish tiles of the fireplace. The portrait of John Knox in stained glass was made in 1853.

➠ *The Netherbow Centre adjoins John Knox House, from which it can be reached directly at ground-floor level.*

Location 11   The Netherbow Centre

45 High Street

❖ Open Monday to Saturday 10am to 5pm. ❖ Admission free.

This arts centre, operated by the Church of Scotland, was opened in 1972. Ever-changing exhibitions of contemporary works are held and a small theatre is incorporated. A bronze sign on the High Street wall of the building depicts the lost Netherbow Port, which stood nearby until it was demolished in 1764. Built in 1513, this was one of the six gates in the city wall; its location on what was then the eastern perimeter of Edinburgh marked the boundary with the Burgh of Canongate. The gate's exact position is indicated by brass studs in the road outside (beside the traffic lights). The gate's bell of 1621 is displayed in the centre's patio garden.

➠ *Exit right and return westward to Paisley Close. Cross to the south side of High Street, where an evocative sign proclaims the Museum of Childhood.*

Location 12   Museum of Childhood

42 High Street

❖ Open Monday to Saturday 10am to 5pm (Sundays during the Festival 2pm to 5pm). ❖ Admission free.

Founded by Patrick Murray in 1955, the museum occupies two storeys of the 18th-century rear wing of the building, which was remodelled internally to house it. Many exhibits come from the private collection of Murray (1908–81), who served as an Edinburgh town councillor; he claimed to dislike children, and remained a bachelor all his life. Soon after it had opened, the museum, the first of its kind, was inundated with gifts from all over the world, and its collection of dolls is still unequalled. In addition to dolls, exhibits in the five galleries include soldiers, toy trains, games, vintage slot machines, puppets, cars, bicycles and children's books.

➠ *Itinerary 5 continues from this point.*

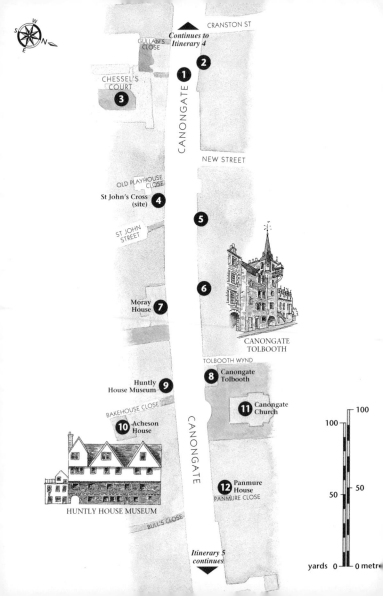

CRANSTON ST

Continues to
Itinerary 4

GULLAN'S
CLOSE

CANONGATE

① ②

CHESSEL'S
COURT

③

NEW STREET

OLD PLAYHOUSE
CLOSE

St John's Cross
(site) ④

⑤

ST JOHN
STREET

⑥

Moray
House ⑦

CANONGATE
TOLBOOTH

TOLBOOTH WYND

⑧ Canongate
Tolbooth

Huntly
House Museum ⑨

CANONGATE

BAKEHOUSE CLOSE

⑪ Canongate
Church

Acheson
House ⑩

Panmure ⑫ House

PANMURE CLOSE

HUNTLY HOUSE MUSEUM

BULL'S CLOSE

Itinerary 5
continues

100 ⌐ 100

100

50 ⌐ 50

yards 0 ⌐ 0 metre

ITINERARY 5

The Royal Mile: Canongate

Huntly House Museum – Canongate Tolbooth –
Canongate Church – White Horse Close

Canongate suffered from a great deal of iconoclastic demolition and
rebuilding between its 19th-century decline and the end of World War II.
In consequence, particularly at the east end, it has a less homogeneous
appearance than High Street, and many apparently ancient buildings have
been greatly remodelled or rebuilt as reproductions – even complete fakes.
The locations of greatest interest to most will be found west of Canongate
Church.

Timing: *As only two museums, which conveniently face each other, and one church lie on
the route, fine weather is advantageous. However, some may wish to continue to the Palace
of Holyroodhouse and Dynamic Earth (Itinerary 10) if time permits.*

Start: *The itinerary continues directly from Itinerary 4, beginning on the east side of
Canongate's junction with Cranston Street.*

Location 1   Canongate

In 1140, twelve years after he had founded the Monastery of the Holy Rood,
David I gave its canons permission to create and administer their own burgh adjacent to Edinburgh, which became known as Canongate. The name refers not to a
gateway but to the route that the canons had taken on foot (gait) from their
abbey church to Edinburgh Castle, in which they had initially been domiciled. In
spite of several extensions to Edinburgh's wall it never encompassed the Burgh of
Canongate, and Holyrood remained undefended by external fortifications
throughout its history.

Due to Holyrood's growing importance as a royal residence, the thoroughfare of
Canongate soon attracted members of the nobility, many of whom built their
town houses close to the abbey. In contrast to Edinburgh, gardens were large, and
orchards flourished, adding to the new burgh's popularity. At the Reformation,
with the suppression of the abbey the responsibility for administering the Burgh
of Canongate passed to laymen.

After James VI (James I of England) vacated Holyrood for London in 1603,
Canongate gradually lost its fashionable status: grand houses remained empty, and

tradesmen migrated elsewhere. The fate of the street was sealed when Edinburgh's
New Town took shape in the late 18th century, and within fifty years its properties had degenerated into light-industrial slums. Shortly before World War II, haphazard reconstruction of Canongate's decayed buildings began, but wholehearted
conservation and restoration were not the guiding principles, scant regard being
paid to historical accuracy. Fortunately, postwar restoration, particularly in recent
years, has been much more sympathetic.

On the north side of Canongate, just east of its junction with Cranston Street, a
modern building, No. 267 (currently the Reform Restaurant), is known as
Morocco Land.

➠ *Cross to the south side of Canongate, from where the building's one point of interest
may be better appreciated.*

Location 2   Morocco Land

267 Canongate

The building is a reconstruction, minus the top storey, of an early 18th-century
tenement that stood nearby. It is the 1957 work of architect Robert Hurd, who
was responsible for much of the sympathetic postwar development at this end of
the street. The half-length stone figure of a 'Moor', from the earlier tenement, has
been set in the facade of the present building, left of its first- and second-floor
windows. Allegedly, Andrew Gray, after being sentenced to death in Edinburgh for
rioting, escaped to Morocco, where he prospered. Disguised as a Moor, Gray
returned to discover that his cousin, a daughter of the Lord Provost, had caught
the plague. She was living with her father in the Canongate tenement, which
Gray visited, successfully administering a cure to the girl: eventually they married
and lived there. By tradition, the Moor's head commemorates Gray's exploit, but a
much less romantic explanation of the carving is that it was a tradesman's sign.

➠ *Remain on the south side of Canongate and proceed westward to the arcades of Nos
234–40 Canongate, behind which lies Chessel's Court.*

Location 3   Chessel's Court

On the west side of the court, right, survives the colourfully rendered building
within which the Excise House was established in the late 18th century. It was
here that Deacon Brodie was recognised in the course of committing burglary.

➠ *Return to Canongate, right. First right Old Playhouse Close.*

The name of this close records a theatre that stood here 1747–67 in spite of objections by the clergy. Sarah Siddons performed in the Playhouse on several occasions.

Beside the entrance to the close a wall plaque on No 196 commemorates the St John's Cross.

Location 4   St John's Cross (site)

Canongate

Cobbles in the form of a Maltese Cross, set in the centre of the road outside No. 196, indicate the location of the standing Cross of St John that marked the boundary between Edinburgh and the Canongate estate that the Knights of the Order of St John owned in the Middle Ages. It was at this point that Charles I, on his first visit to Edinburgh in 1633, was ceremonially greeted by the Lord Provost, whom he promptly knighted.

➤ *Cross to the north side of Canongate.*

Location 5   Shoemakers Land

197 Canongate

The building, which was completed in 1954, marked the beginning of Robert Hurd's award-winning Tolbooth Area Redevelopment. Prior to Hurd's reconstruction, a medieval tenement on the site had itself been rebuilt by the Incorporation of Cordiners (shoemakers) in 1725. From the 1725 building, an inscribed panel carved with a gilded crown above a shoemaker's knife has been inserted above the doorway.

➤ *Continue eastward.*

Location 6   Bible Land

185 Canongate

This tenement was erected by the Cordiners in 1677, but its street frontage has been almost entirely rebuilt. Above the door the dated cartouche bearing a grotesque head and the crowned shoemaker's knife, emblem of the Cordiners, flanked by cherubs' heads, has been retained from the original facade. Part of the inscription on the open scrolled book below, and also original, was inspired by Psalm 133, which is why the development was named Bible Land.

➤ *Remain on the north side of Canongate, from where the long facade of Moray House, directly opposite, may best be appraised.*

Location 7   Moray House

Canongate

Moray House, one of Canongate's most impressive town houses, was built around 1625 for Mary, Dowager Countess of Home. Her daughter Margaret, who inherited the property in 1643, became Countess of Moray, and the house still bears the name of the Moray family, in whose possession it remained until the mid-19th century.

Flanking the gate to the courtyard are two enormous obelisks. The lodge, right, is a 19th-century addition. Immediately east of the gate, the high-gabled block with a balcony is presumably the original mansion built by Lady Home as her arms are carved above the central window. Many blocked doors and windows at ground-floor level will be noted. Stretching eastward, the long wing of the house was probably added by Margaret later in the 17th century.

Charles I is believed to have visited the house, and Oliver Cromwell certainly lodged there on two occasions. By tradition, in 1650, while the Marquess of Argyle was celebrating his son's wedding day in the building, his hated political rival, the Marquess of Montrose, was marched past Moray House on his way to trial. Observing this, Argyle and his wedding guests are said to have spat at the poor man from the balcony. Another tradition pertaining to the mansion is that the commissioners originally proposed to sign the Act of Union in its summer house, but so many Scotsmen opposed it that to avoid trouble a less prominent venue – a High Street basement – was chosen.

⇒ *Continue eastward passing, first right, Sugarhouse Close, to the Huntly House Museum.*

The exterior of Canongate Tolbooth, opposite, on the north side of Canongate, is best appreciated from outside the museum.

Location 8   Canongate Tolbooth (The People's Story Museum)

Canongate

❖ Open Monday to Saturday 10am to 5pm (Sundays during the Festival 2pm to 5pm). ❖ Admission free.

When built in 1591 on the site of an earlier Tolbooth, this was the administrative centre of Canongate Burgh. The tower was constructed first, followed by the courthouse range to the east. Attached to the tower's west face is a tenement of

1581, which was incorporated later in the Tolbooth but which has accommodated a tavern since 1821.

With its conical spire and turrets, the influence of contemporary French architecture on the picturesque tower is noticeable. Gunloops inserted in the sides of the turrets give the building an appearance of half-hearted fortification, but the main aim of these was to impress the onlookers, particularly those living in neighbouring Edinburgh, with the importance of the burgh.

Above the archway to Old Tolbooth Wynd, a stone c.1591 is inscribed SLB (commemorating Sir Lewis Bellenden, the leader of the burgh at the time), followed by 'Patriae et Posteris' (the burgh's motto). The clock extending over Canongate is dated 1884, the year of its erection.

Canongate Tolbooth

The courthouse range, in particular its roof and ground floor, was somewhat altered during late 19th-century restoration; its west gable is dated 1875. At the same time, the framed coat of arms of the burgh was set up in the centre of the wall; a Latin inscription extols justice and compassion.

In addition to a courtroom, the Tolbooth's courthouse originally accommodated the council's debating chamber, administrative offices, a centre for the collection of tolls (taxes), and the burgh's prison.

➠ *Cross to the north side of Canongate and enter the building.*

The Canongate Tolbooth now houses The People's Story, a museum in which the lives of Edinburghers from the 18th century to the present are described: an apt complement to the Huntly House Museum opposite.

➠ *Exit from the building, remaining on the north side of Canongate to view the exterior of Huntly House, opposite.*

Location 9   Huntly House Museum

142 Canongate

❖ Open Monday to Saturday 10am to 5pm (Sundays during the Festival 2pm to 5pm). ❖ Admission free.

Spread over a rambling complex of venerable buildings, this splendid museum brings the history of Edinburgh to life.

Huntly House, the core of the museum, is the triple-gabled building, incorporating the entrance to Bakehouse Close, that adjoins the small 17th-century house through which the museum is entered. Three early 16th-century dwellings were combined in 1570 by John Acheson to provide a spacious – but never grand – house, which appears to have acquired its impressive-sounding name from George, 1st Marquess of Huntly, who temporarily lodged there in 1636.

After more than a century of decline, Huntly House was purchased by the City of Edinburgh in 1924, and converted to a museum. The two upper storeys are modern replicas of a 1667 addition to the building.

➠ *Cross to the museum, which is entered from the building immediately left of Bakehouse Close.*

Interior

A surprising number of plain 17th-century fireplaces and areas of panelling original to the house have survived.

Those who have been exploring The Royal Mile will be able to gain some idea of its 17th-century appearance from a fascinating scale model. Particularly surprising is the colourful paintwork of the rendered properties, in striking contrast to the almost uniformly dark grey stonework of present-day Edinburgh.

Field-Marshal Earl Haig, commander of the British army in France during World War I, was born in Edinburgh's fashionable Charlotte Square, and two rooms exhibit memorabilia of the man whom many now hold to be chiefly responsible for the carnage of the trenches. A popular feature of the museum is its period rooms, which give a taste of domestic life in Edinburgh throughout the centuries. Other exhibits of interest are the original Covenant, memorabilia connected with Greyfriars Bobby and a collection of Edinburgh glass and silver.

➠ *Exit right to the adjacent building.*

Location 10 Acheson House

140 Canongate

Sir Archibald Acheson, Charles I's Secretary of State for Scotland, commissioned this as his town house in 1633. When built, existing properties stood between Acheson House and Canongate, but these have since been removed, and what was originally the north side wall is now, after remodelling, the main frontage.

Acheson House was restored in 1937 for the 4th Marquess of Bute, who was responsible for saving a number of derelict Canongate properties. Above the Canongate entrance is the inscription 'O Lord in thee is all my traist (trust)'; the doorway came from a demolished building in Anchor Close. Due to the high wall and trees in the garden, little can be seen of the Canongate facade – even by crossing to the north side of the road.

➡ *Return westward. First left Bakehouse Close. Proceed through the archway.*

On the east side of the close, left, the original frontage to Acheson House may be glimpsed behind its courtyard's wall.

The stair tower's crowstepped gable, left, was added in 1937, based on a design by the original architect that had never been executed.

Two gables, right of this tower, respectively bear the monograms AA and MH of Archibald Acheson and his wife Margaret Hamilton.

To the south, the doorway dated 1679 was brought from a demolished property.

➡ *Return to Canongate and cross to the north side.*

Location 11 Canongate Church

Canongate

In 1687 James VII (James II of England) decided to convert the church of the former Abbey of Holyrood into a chapel for members of the Order of the Thistle, a plan that was never realised due to his deposition. Since the Reformation, the abbey church had served as the parish church of Canongate, and the present building was constructed specifically to house its congregation. Ironically, the parish of Canongate Church now incorporates the Palace of Holyroodhouse, and the sovereign worships here when residing in Edinburgh.

James Smith designed the church in 1688, the year in which James VII was replaced as monarch by joint rulers: his daughter Mary II and the Dutch William III.

Canongate Church

Exterior

It is tempting to speculate whether the Dutch appearance of Canongate Church, with its deep windows and fanciful gable, specifically indicated respect for the new king, whose arms are carved above the circular window. Entirely classical, however, is the portico, with its wide pediment and side doors, which are also pedimented. Above the main entrance, an inscribed panel confirms the granting of Thomas Moodie's mortification of 1649. Moodie, whose arms appear above the plaque, had actually mortified (donated) money for a church to be built in the Grassmarket.

➠ *Enter the church.*

Canongate Church opened for Protestant services in 1691, but its short transepts and shallow, apsed chancel, which are more suited to the celebration of Mass, may have been specified by James VII and laid out at an early stage.

Apart from the vestry's 17th-century benefactors board, no fixtures or fittings in the church predate the 19th century.

➠ *Exit left and proceed to the east wall of the churchyard.*

Canongate Churchyard was laid out in 1688 and many renowned parishioners who died in the 18th and 19th centuries are buried within.

Against the wall, facing the nave of the church, a bronze portrait medallion and the name Clarinda are all that identify the famous mistress of Robert Burns. Their relationship was not discovered until after her death in 1841, at the age of 82, when the poet's many letters to her were discovered. Clarinda's real name was Mrs Agnes Maclehose; her husband had emigrated to Jamaica, leaving her with their two children to care for. It was Clarinda to whom Burns referred in his moving verse:

> *Had we never lov'd sae kindly*
> *Had we never lov'd sae blindly*
> *Never met – or never parted –*
> *We had ne'er been broken-hearted.*

The couple parted for the last time in 1791, five years before the poet's death.

➠ *Proceed clockwise around the church to the south wall of the churchyard's west sector.*

A monument to the Scottish economist Adam Smith (1723–90) incorporates a small, sculpted portrait.

➠ *Follow the wall northward.*

Buried in front of the wall is the poet Robert Fergusson (1751–74), whose work had a great influence on Robert Burns. On finding the grave uncared for in 1780, Burns commissioned the present headstone to be made, and composed its fond dedication.

➠ *Return to Canongate, left. Fourth left, Little Lochend Close runs northward through the arcade immediately before No. 103 and a terrace of shops.*

Location 12   Panmure House

Little Lochend Close

Built with crowstepped gables towards the end of the 17th century as the town house of the Jacobite Earl of Panmure, this mansion is of interest chiefly due to its ownership by the political economist Adam Smith. He purchased the house in 1778, two years after the publication of his *An Inquiry into the Nature and Causes of the Wealth of Nations,* a treatise that was chiefly responsible for its author's own wealth and enduring fame. Adam Smith died at Panmure House in 1790.

Immediately left, the 18th-century Cadell House faces eastward, and like Panmure House is detached.

➠ *Return to Canongate, left. Second left Reid's Court.*

Canongate Manse was built around 1700, but its wings were added later in the 18th century. The house ceased to be the manse of Canongate in 1832 but was reinstated as such after restoration in 1959.

➠ *Return to Canongate, left, and continue eastward, passing Jenny Ha's bar, to No. 65 Canongate.*

A Canongate wall plaque on a modern building of no intrinsic interest commemorates the site of Golfer's Land, a tenement built in the 17th century. By tradition, in 1679 shoemaker John Paterson, an accomplished golfer, was chosen by the Duke of York, later James VII, to partner him in a foursome to be played on the links at nearby Leith. The duke and his partner won the match, due primarily to the skill of Paterson, who was generously rewarded. With the money, Bailie John Paterson, as he later became, was able to build his Canongate tenement, which became known as Golfer's Land. Above the plaque, the bronze coat of arms has been copied from a stone set in the original building. At the base are set the praiseworthy words 'For and sure I hate no person'.

➠ *Continue eastward. First left Galloway's Entry.*

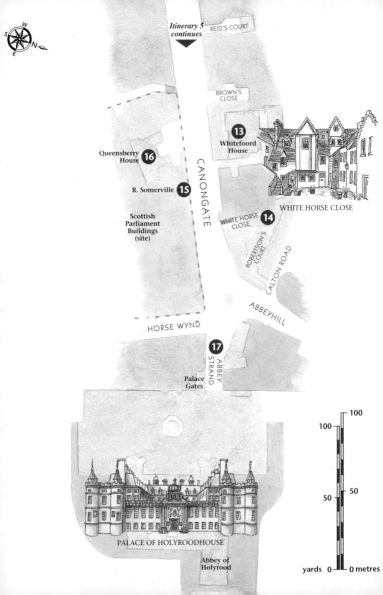

Itinerary 5 continues

W N S E

REID'S COURT

BROWN'S CLOSE

13
Whiteford
House

WHITE HORSE CLOSE

Queensberry **16**
House

CANONGATE

R. Somerville **15**

Scottish
Parliament
Buildings
(site)

WHITE HORSE **14**
CLOSE

ROBERTSON'S
COURT

CALTON ROAD

ABBEYHILL

HORSE WYND

17

ABBEY STRAND

Palace
Gates

PALACE OF HOLYROODHOUSE

Abbey of
Holyrood

100

100

50

50

yards 0   0 metres

Location 13   Whitefoord House

Galloway's Entry is flanked by stone piers, formerly the gateposts of Whitefoord House that lies ahead.

Sir John Whitefoord commissioned Robert Mylne to design this three-storey mansion in 1766 on the site of Seton Palace, in which Lord Darnley had lodged prior to his marriage with Mary, Queen of Scots. As an indication of Canongate's dilapidated state, by the mid-19th century Whitefoord House accommodated an iron foundry, and internally only its stairway has survived. After World War II, Whitefoord House was remodelled and extended to provide the Scottish Veterans Residences for ex-servicemen. Alterations made included the unimpressive mock-Georgian extension to the east.

Callander House was attached to the west side of Whitefoord House for Sir John Callander, also around 1766, but its original appearance has greatly changed.

➠ *Return to Canongate and continue eastward to the modern arcade that provides the frontage to White Horse Close, which is reached from the passage beside No. 27.*

Location 14   White Horse Close

In spite of its obviously fake, filmset appearance, this picturesque corner of 'old' Edinburgh will charm most visitors. In the late 17th century, the White Horse Inn was built at the north end of the close as a staging post for the London coach. The philanthropic Dr Barbour and his sister purchased the entire close in 1889 and reconstructed it to provide homes for the low-paid. Even more whole-sale reconstruction took place in 1962, when the close was modernised and its picturesque nature amplified. Although some stonework has been incorporated in the rebuilding, most structures are of rendered brick.

At the north end, where the 'vernacular' prettiness evokes a Walt Disney cartoon, a gable's datestone is inscribed 1623. It is said that at one time the date quoted was 1523, but realising that this was stretching a knowledgeable visitor's gullibility a bit too far, the present date was cut in 1930. Below the stone it is admitted that rebuilding took place in 1962. At the top of the steps, a plaque records that the original White Horse Inn was 'probably built by Laurence Ord'.

➠ *Exit from White Horse Close to Canongate, right. Cross to the south side and return westward to R. Somerville at No. 82, directly opposite Golfer's Land.*

Location 15   R. Somerville

82 Canongate

Visitors are welcome to enter this shop, within which are displayed playing cards, all of them for sale. More than 2,000 packs are kept in stock, the most valuable being complete examples from the 17th century. Surprisingly, there is no name in English for collectors of playing cards; *The Times* once held a competition to create one, but no suggestion was considered worthy.

The facade of the shop's crowstep-gabled building is a 1953 replica of the 17th-century home of Nisbet of Dirleton. Nisbet, a member of the judiciary, was renowned for the harsh sentences that he meted out to Covenanters. A lintel from the original house, inscribed in Latin and dated 1619, has been reused. Another reused stone to its right (above the doorway to No. 84) bears inscriptions in Latin and English and is also dated 1619.

➠ *Continue eastward, passing Reid's Close, to Queensberry House.*

In front of the building, another of the Royal Mile's wells is dated 1817.

Location 16   Queensberry House

Canongate

In 1999, this building, formerly the Queensberry Hospital, was incorporated in the area destined for the new Scottish Parliament, and its original external appearance is to be restored. Although the mansion was commissioned by Lord Hatton in 1681, on its completion five years later he sold it immediately to the 1st Duke of Queensberry, whose name it bears. Queensberry House was converted into flats in the 18th century, but soon became an army barracks. In 1832 the building served as a People's Refuge, no doubt contributing to the down-and-out aspect of Canongate.

A grizzly tale relates to the house during the ownership of James, son of the 1st Duke of Queensberry and prime mover in the controversial campaign for Scotland's union with England. While James was canvassing signatures of support, it is said that his eldest son, Lord Drumlanrig, murdered a kitchen boy, whose body he then cooked and ate. Although Drumlanrig was undoubtedly unbalanced, most Scots were strongly averse to the proposed union, and some may have taken their revenge on the Queensberry dynasty by maliciously inventing the tale.

➠ *Continue eastward to No. 5, Russell House.*

Stones forming a circle in the road outside Russell House, a 17th-century tenement, mark the site of the Girth Cross, another of Edinburgh's numerous locations for public executions. Primarily, however, the cross marked the western boundary of Holyrood Abbey's precinct.

➡ *Cross the roundabout to Abbey Strand, the short thoroughfare ahead, which leads to the Palace of Holyroodhouse.*

Location 17 Abbey Strand

Until the roundabout was created, Abbey Strand, located within Holyrood Abbey's precinct, continued westward to link directly with Canongate. A small brass 's' set in the centre of the road at the point where the cobblestones meet the tarmac commemorates sanctuary from arrest for civil crimes within the area of the abbey precinct, a common practice in medieval Europe. Sanctuary has never been officially abolished at Holyrood, although no invocation of it has been tested in law. Formerly, the punishment in Scotland for debt was imprisonment and, in order to avoid this, many debtors took advantage of sanctuary. Those who were able to obtain sufficient funds resided in Abbey Strand, where they were referred to as the 'Abbey Lairds'. No arrests could be made anywhere in Scotland on a Sunday, which was the only day on which those claiming sanctuary could leave the precinct with impunity. The area of sanctuary at Holyrood, which included all of Holyrood Park, was established shortly after the monastery's foundation in 1128, and remained effective until Scotland abolished imprisonment for debt in 1880.

➡ *Proceed to the north side of Abbey Strand.*

The rendered four-storey building was constructed around 1500 as a three-storey-plus-attic tenement, which accommodated two families on each floor. First-floor windows are original, but those on the second floor appear to have been remodelled around 1690; the present upper storey was built in 1916.

External steps lead to the first floor of the tenement's picturesque two-storey extension, built to the east around 1690. It is surmounted by three crowstepped gables, and continues around the east side of the tenement block, creating an L-shape. The ground floor, including the archway, was rebuilt in 1935; it incorporates the Abbey Sanctuary Information Centre and bookshop.

Ahead lies the Palace of Holyroodhouse and nearby, to the south, Dynamic Earth and the new Scottish Parliament building – due for completion in late 2001. These locations, together with Calton Hill, are covered by Itinerary 10.

Old Town South-west

National Library of Scotland – Victoria Street –
Magdalen Chapel – Grassmarket

This itinerary primarily explores the sector of Old Town south of The Royal Mile and west of George IV Bridge. Although it is not lengthy, there are museums within the Bank of Scotland, Scottish Parliament Visitors Centre and National Library of Scotland; the Magdalen Chapel is probably Edinburgh's most interesting medieval religious building to have survived. Many will also spend some time in Victoria Street's fascinating shops and the historic Grassmarket.

Timing: *As most of the route is in the open air, fine weather is desirable.*

Start: *The west end of Market Street at the top of Playfair Steps and The Mound.*

Location 1   Black Watch Regiment Memorial

Market Street

Commemorated are the members of the Black Watch Regiment who died in the South African 'Boer' War (1899–1902); the kilted bronze figure was cast by William Birnie Rhind in 1910.

➡ *From the monument cross the road to Mound Place.*

Location 2   Church of Scotland's Assembly Hall and New College

Mound Place

The complex was designed as New College by William Playfair for the Church of Scotland, 1845–50. High, octagonal towers in mock-Tudor style flank the vaulted archway to the symmetrical quadrangle. Playfair set its axis on his Royal Scottish Academy below. Almost on the same axis to the south, but not quite, rises the black spire of the former Tolbooth Church (now The Hub), where the Church of Scotland held its assemblies until 1929.

The bronze figure in the quadrangle, left, of John Knox, by John Hutchinson, was cast in 1895.

On the east side, left, the original Free High Church of the college was converted to the library in 1936. Most of the complex accommodates Edinburgh University's New College Faculty of Divinity.

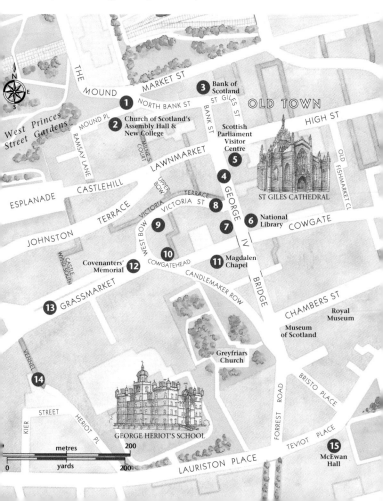

Steps on the south side of the quadrangle ahead lead to the Assembly Hall, which was completed in 1859 by David Bryce, the architect Playfair having died two years earlier.

Each May, ministers of the Church of Scotland come to the hall from all over the country to spend one week debating and decreeing church policy. The Moderator chairs the session and, if unable to attend personally, the sovereign is represented by the Lord High Commissioner. On the first day, delegates march in procession along The Royal Mile from Holyroodhouse to their hall, accompanied by bag-pipes and drummers. It has been agreed that Parliament will relocate during this week throughout its occupancy of the Assembly Hall.

➡ *If the debating chamber is to be visited at this stage (see page 29), exit from the court-yard, right. First right, steps ascend to Milne's Court. Access to the debating chamber is via the temporary building, at the top of the steps, right.*

➡ *Alternatively, if the debating chamber has already been viewed, return to Mound Place, turn right, pass Milne's Court and continue to North Bank Street where, on the north side, the Head Office of the Bank of Scotland faces Bank Street.*

Location 3   Bank of Scotland

Bank Street

❖ Museum on the Mound: Open June to September, Monday to Friday during banking hours. ❖ Admission free.

The building combines schemes by two 19th-century architects that are separated by more than half a century. When it was founded in 1695 the bank first leased premises off High Street, later moving to a Lawnmarket close. In 1801 the site was purchased for the present building, which Robert Reid and Richard Crichton were commissioned to design. Problematically, the land fell steeply to the north, and the 98 ft (30 m) disparity in levels resulted in a disproportionately high north facade, which the architects tried, unsuccessfully, to disguise with a screen wall.

In 1863, David Bryce was appointed to extend and remodel the bank. Although he completely altered the north facade by emphasising its height, few changes were made to Reid's North Bank Street facade. Viewed from Bank Street, howev-er, the new dome is the only significant difference, Reid's version having been much shallower. Bryce based his Baroque design on the dome of Santi Luca e Martina in Rome, by Pietro da Cortona.

The flanking wings, both Bryce's additions, are linked with the central block by single-storey ranges. A view at night of the floodlit building from Bank Street is most impressive.

Located in the basement, the Museum on the Mound traces the history of the Bank of Scotland. The minting of Scottish coins ended following the Act of Union, but Scottish banknotes continued to be printed, and still are – including,

Princes Street Gardens, looking towards the Church of Scotland's Assembly Hall

unlike in England, the £1 denomination. Of interest to numismatists is the collection of ancient coins, which include Roman specimens, and banknotes, some of them printed by forgers who risked the death penalty if caught. Exhibited is an amusing letter of 1733 to the Dean of the Guild of Edinburgh complaining of the 'nastyness' from tenement windows suffered by the bank's customers on their way to and from the bank when it was located off Lawnmarket.

➠ *At Lawnmarket, Bank Street, right, links with George IV Bridge via the short Melbourne Place.*

Location 4   George IV Bridge

Work began on this bridge in 1829 to provide direct access to Lawnmarket from the south. The structure's name honours George IV, who died in 1830, four years before its completion; the king remained extremely popular in the city, which he had visited in 1822.

Follow the west side of the bridge southward, passing the temporary Scottish Parliament Administration Offices, which occupy the entire block between Lawnmarket and Victoria Street. This typically unsympathetic late-1960s horror was built as the former Lothian Regional Council Headquarters.

➠ *Cross to the east side of the bridge.*

Location 5   Scottish Parliament Committee Chambers and Visitor Centre

George IV Bridge (Melbourne Place)

Completed in 1905 as Midlothian County Council Buildings, the block was designed in a heavy Palladian pastiche style, presumably to complement the much earlier building behind it facing West Parliament Square, of which it is an extension. Visitors wishing to learn about the new Scottish Parliament are presented with information and shown a scale model of the complex.

➠ *Continue southward, remaining on the east side, to the National Library of Scotland.*

Location 6   National Library of Scotland

George IV Bridge

The library was designed in 1936 but not completed until 1955 due to interruption by World War II. The Advocates Library, established in 1682, provided the basis of the library, which was founded in 1925. Of outstanding interest are a Gutenberg Bible of 1455, the last letter written by Mary, Queen of Scots, and Celtic manuscripts. An exhibition room features displays on regularly changing themes.

▪▶ *Exit and cross to the west side of George IV Bridge.*

Location 7 Edinburgh Central Public Library

George IV Bridge

This library, occupying the oldest building of importance on the bridge, was completed in 1890. It is designed in early French Renaissance style, and has a picturesque quality that contrasts with the cold neo-classicism of its neighbours.

Andrew Carnegie, whose name is perpetuated by New York's Carnegie Hall, was born in Dunfermline, and donated a generous sum to establish the library. His bust of 1891 stands in a recess at upper landing level.

Adjacent to the Reference Library's entrance, the doorway, inscribed Tecum habita 1625, was saved from Sir Thomas Hope's mansion in Cowgate when it was demolished for the construction of the library. Another 17th-century doorway from the same mansion, inscribed 'At hospes humo', forms the entrance to the Scottish Library, a section that is located at second basement level.

Of great interest to many visitors is the Edinburgh Library, at mezzanine level, which was created in 1958. Photographs, maps and memorabilia relating to the city's history are displayed.

▪▶ *Return to George IV Bridge, left (there is also an exit from the library to Cowgate at the lower level). First left Victoria Street.*

Location 8 Victoria Street

Although of no great length, Victoria Street, together with its West Bow continuation, is just about everyone's favourite Edinburgh shopping thoroughfare. Picturesquely winding downhill, many Victorian shop fronts have survived, their interiors retaining a naturally venerable appearance without giving the impression of striving to recreate an 'old Edinburgh' effect.

Victoria Street was laid out 1829–34 in connection with the George IV Bridge development. Once the unfortunate modern block has been passed, its north side seems to have changed little since originally built. Although fronted with ashlar stone, the exteriors of the shops are all painted in a variety of colours, which adds to the thoroughfare's liveliness and offers welcome relief from the blackened stonework of so many Edinburgh buildings.

The south side of Victoria Street provides a complete contrast, its east sector being occupied by the bulging India Buildings of 1864 and the Jacobean-style St John's Church of 1840, now converted to the Byzantine Market of small shops. Directly opposite, steps on the north side ascend to Victoria Terrace (see page 29). Due to the steep gradient, properties on the north side, all of which have even numbers, increase in height from one to three storeys as the descent is made.

Before Victoria Street was laid out, West Bow swung dramatically northward approximately opposite Anderson's Close, making an incredibly steep ascent to link with what is now called Upper Bow.

Iain Mellis (No. 30A) retails cheeses produced in the United Kingdom, the range and quality of which staggers even French visitors.

Difficult to miss, Robert Cresser (No. 40) is in some ways the most appealing of all Victoria Street's shops. Brushes and brooms have been sold on the premises since 1833, i.e. when the street first opened – and still are. Zinc buckets and wooden spoons are also sold, but it is the brooms and brushes that dominate, filling the shop and spilling out onto the street.

Location 9   West Bow

By tradition, the name of West Bow refers to the distance that an arrow from a bow could be fired from the castle; however, a more likely source was the street's original double bend, or bow. Apparently it was formerly pronounced 'bough'.

Marking the north end of West Bow, No. 87, the building occupied by Clarkson's the jewellers, was specifically designed in 1850 to provide a link between the newly laid out Victoria Street and what remained of West Bow. Sympathetically, although faced with ashlar stone to match the houses in Victoria Street, it has also been given a stepped gable to conform with the 17th-century style of West Bow.

No. 89 has a mid-19th-century shop front, but the building itself dates from the late 17th century. Its small, crowstepped gable is provided with holes to encourage doves or pigeons to nest within; the householders were not pigeon fanciers but enjoyed a good pigeon pie.

The street's only 18th-century shop front to survive, at No. 93, is dated 1729 above its door.

A crowstepped gable above Nos 101–105 is surmounted by a fleur-de-lis finial, which is dated (rather optimistically) 1561.

Adjoining, No. 107 comprises five storeys and an attic. It retains part of a door lintel inscribed 'God for all his gifts 1616'. Presumably, the words 'Blessed be' had been carved on a missing section.

➠ *Continue ahead to the junction with Grassmarket.*

The West Bow Well was built by Robert Mylne in 1674. Its cast-iron door on the west side, together with the basin, horse trough and carvings by John Rhind, were added in 1861.

➠ *Cross to West Bow's south-east corner.*

At No. 118, The Cook's Bookshop is Scotland's only cookery book specialist. Its owner Clarissa Dickson Wright has achieved fame among tele-belly enthusiasts through her successful *Two Fat Ladies* culinary programmes.

➠ *Exit left Cowgate, and cross the road immediately to Cowgatehead opposite.*

Location 10   Cowgatehead

Three adjacent shops on the south side will interest many: Mr Wood's Fossils (No. 5) sells decorative natural stones in addition to the fossils, mostly of Scottish origin, for which the owner is internationally renowned. Transreal Fiction (No. 7) stocks exactly what its name suggests – science fiction and fantasy books. Wind Things (No. 11) specialises in kites, but also includes puzzles, juggling props and balloons among its wide range of merchandise.

➠ *Continue eastward to Cowgate (ignoring the Candlemaker Row right fork) where, on the right, is a rare Edinburgh example of a religious building that predates the Reformation.*

Location 11   Magdalen Chapel

41 Cowgate

❖ Open Monday to Friday 9.30am - 4pm. Other times by appointment, tel/fax 0131 220-1450.

Built 1541–44 as an almshouse chapel, this small building served as the guildhall of its patrons, the Incorporation of Hammermen, for more than 300 years; it is now the headquarters of the Scottish Reformation Society. Of exceptional interest within are four heraldic roundels, the only examples of pre-Reformation stained glass to have survived in Scotland.

Mitchell Macquhane, a wealthy member of the influential Hammermen's

Incorporation, who died in 1537, bequeathed a sum of money for building the chapel together with accommodation for a chaplain and seven 'bedesmen' (i.e. bedsmen: impoverished gentlemen in need of lodgings). However, it was not until Macquhane's widow Janet Rynd donated a much greater sum in 1541 that work on the project could proceed.

Completed in 1544, the chapel was dedicated to Mary Magdalen in honour of Mary of Guise and Lorraine, then regent for her young daughter Mary, Queen of Scots. An adjacent almshouse opened three years later.

Undoubtedly the most significant event in the chapel's history occurred in 1560, when the First General Assembly of the Reformed Church of Scotland met to outline its policy; among the forty-two commissioners attending was John Knox.

Exterior

The tower was added to the front of the chapel in 1625, but its doorway and second-stage windows were rebuilt in Tudor style in 1817. A carving above the door, made in 1615 but transferred here from the forecourt's entrance in 1649, depicts the initials and arms of Mitchell Macquhane and Janet Rynd separated by the Hammermen's emblem and flanked by a bedesman and a hammerman; the date, 1553, commemorates the year of Janet Rynd's death, following which the Incorporation of Hammermen took over the foundation's patronage.

Stretching eastward from the tower, the mock-Tudor facade of the two-storey Committee Room was added by Richard Crichton in 1817. This is matched on the west side by a building added in 1878; the bedesmen's accommodation was demolished in 1875.

Interior

An original, mid 15th-century doorway provides the entrance from the tower to the chapel.

The brass chandelier was made in 1813 by an apprentice as an 'essay' piece, in order to gain his acceptance into the Incorporation of Hammermen.

Walls are lined with three tiers of arched 'brods' (boards) on which are recorded gifts made to the chapel between 1555 and 1813. The name and occupation of each benefactor is followed by the donation given in various currencies, fittings or building materials.

The two curved tiers of seating and their wrought-iron railing were made around 1725; painted on the backs of the lower tier are the Hammermen's arms.

In the south-east corner of the chapel, the tombstone of Janet Rynd is carved with her coat of arms.

Set in the south wall's central window, and made specifically for the newly-built chapel around 1544, the four roundels are the only examples of pre-Reformation stained glass in Scotland to have survived. Presumably they were spared because they are heraldic, and do not depict saints or biblical scenes, then considered heretical. The top left panel comprises the Royal Arms of Scotland; to the right of this are the arms of Regent Mary of Guise and Lorraine. The bottom left roundel displays the arms of Mitchell Macquhane; to the right of this are the arms of Janet Rynd.

The former doorway to the bedesmen's accommodation stood in the centre of the west wall until it was filled in 1993. On this wall are an early 18th-century panel painted with the arms of Edinburgh, and above it an inscribed stone panel dated 1624, which invokes the Lord's blessing on the Hammermen.

➠ *Exit from the chapel, left, and return westward to Grassmarket. Cross to the island in the road facing West Bow.*

Location 12   Covenanters' Memorial

Grassmarket

A stainless-steel plaque commemorates almost 100 Covenanters who were publicly hanged in Grassmarket between 1661 and 1688. Since 1937, cobblestones have marked the exact location of the scaffold on which the gallows was erected.

Location 13   Grassmarket

Even though only a handful of its buildings predate the 19th century, Grassmarket's north side, directly overlooked by the castle, still presents a picturesque sight – the south side is another matter.

Grassmarket, still Old Town's most extensive open space, gained its name in 1477, when James III granted a charter for a weekly market, originally of hay and corn, to be held there every Friday, a tradition that continued until 1911, when the venue was changed to west Edinburgh.

The south side has been dominated by unsympathetic modern buildings since 1969, when the enormous Mountbatten Building was constructed for Heriot-Watt University on the site of the Corn Exchange.

On the north side, although few buildings predate the second half of the 19th century, the general appearance of Grassmarket's more venerable past has been retained, with crowstepped gables prominent. The name of Maggie Dickson's pub, at No. 92, commemorates Margaret Dickson, a popular fishwife who lived in High Street. After her husband had abandoned her, she was seduced by the son of a publican and became pregnant; the child was born prematurely and died. Illegally trying to hide the body, Maggie was discovered and subsequently hanged at Grassmarket on 2 September 1724. At the graveyard, however, her cries from the coffin indicated that she was still alive; no further action was taken and 'Half Hangit (Hanged) Maggie' lived for another forty years.

Above the doorway to No. 76, a stone bearing a religious tract is dated 1634; this was probably retained from one of the two tenements that previously stood here.

The White Hart Inn, at No. 36, occupies part of a late 18th-century double tenement, possibly Grassmarket's oldest surviving building. On the last visit of Robert Burns to Edinburgh, in 1791, during which he finally parted from 'Clarinda', the poet is believed to have lodged at the newly-built inn. William Wordsworth was another poet to stay at the inn, accompanied by his sister Dorothy during their tour of Scotland in 1803. The popular tale that Dorothy asked for her room to be changed for one with a better view of the public executions cannot be true as these had been transferred from Grassmarket to Lawnmarket in 1784.

West Port continues from the far end of Grassmarket. In a lodging house in one of its closes, since demolished, body-snatchers Burke and Hare lived and committed their grizzly 19th-century murders.

➠ *From Grassmarket's south-west corner ascend the steps of Vennel, which rise steeply.*

Location 14   Vennel

Vennel leads to a watchtower, the only significant existing remnant of Edinburgh's Flodden Wall, which was constructed in 1514, a year after the English defeated the Scots at the Battle of Flodden Field. The wall encompassed the burghs of Grassmarket and Cowgate for the first time, giving them, as well as Edinburgh itself, protection from an English attack, and also acting as a deterrent to smugglers.

Immediately left, at the top of the steps, the battlemented south-west watchtower of the wall is built of pink and gold stone rubble. A single aperture, known as a crosslet gunloop, through which a gun could be fired, pierces its north face; the west face retains a pair of gunloops and bears an explanatory plaque. As much of the Flodden Wall comprised strengthened garden enclosures and the backs of houses, little of it has survived.

The section of wall that follows, known as Telfer's Wall, was erected in 1620 by mason John Tailefer, primarily to enclose the ten acres of land that had been recently incorporated within the city's boundaries; it now skirts the west grounds of George Heriot's School.

➤ *Continue ahead. First left, Lauriston Place.*

Lauriston Place was laid out in 1762 after the watchtowers in Telfer's Wall that stood in its path had been demolished.

➤ *Remain on the north side.*

Overlooking Lauriston Place, the gatehouse of George Heriot's School was built by William Playfair in 1829. Playfair here produces pastiche Jacobean work. North of the gatehouse can be seen the old school (page 91), which is genuinely Jacobean, being designed around 1628.

➤ *Continue ahead to the crossroads, where Lauriston Place becomes Teviot Place. On the south side, right, stands the domed McEwan Hall.*

Location 15   McEwan Hall

Teviot Place

The hall was built by Sir Robert Rowand Anderson in 1897 as part of Edinburgh University's Medical School complex. The D-shaped building has been described as 'a magnificent petrified blancmange' and a 'glorious and elaborately iced cake', both of which seem apt, but it would have been even more splendid if the statues intended for the niches in the buttresses had been made.

The building is primarily the ceremonial hall of the University of Edinburgh; due to a long echo it has proved unsuitable for most types of music to be played, although choral and organ works, which are less detrimentally affected by echo, are performed to general satisfaction.

➤ *Proceed to the south side of the hall.*

Forming part of the same complex, the Italian-style Reid Concert Hall predates the McEwan Hall by forty years. As its acoustics are far better, more varied concerts can be held. The Edinburgh University Collection of Historical Musical Instruments, located in the building, comprises around 2000 items dating from the 17th century to the present.

➤ *Return to Teviot Place, left. First right Forest Road. Second left, Greyfriars Place branches left to Candlemakers Row, where, at the acute angle formed by its junction with George IV Bridge and Chambers Street, stands the Greyfriars Bobby Fountain (Itinerary 7).*

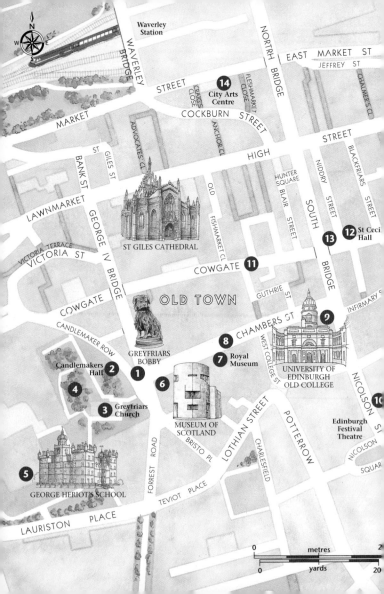

Old Town South-east

Greyfriars Bobby Fountain – Greyfriars Church – Museum of Scotland –
Royal Museum – University of Edinburgh Old College

Locations on this itinerary lie to the south and east of George IV Bridge.
A great deal of time can be spent in the new Museum of Scotland and the
Royal Museum, with which it is linked.

Timing: *The two large museums, Greyfriars Church and Edinburgh University's Old
College lie within a short distance of each other, which is particularly convenient if the
weather is wet.*

Start: *The south end of George IV Bridge at its junction with Candlemaker Row.*

Location 1	Greyfriars Bobby Fountain

Candlemaker Row/George IV Bridge/Chambers Street

The life-size bronze of Bobby, the world-famous Skye terrier, embellishes a public
water fountain, the work of William Brodie, unveiled in 1873 (the granite bowl
no longer holds water); it was commissioned by Baroness Burdett-Coutts in 1872,
the year in which Bobby died.

On his death in 1858, John Gray, an Edinburgh policeman (not a shepherd, as is
generally believed), was interred in Greyfriars Churchyard, and his dog, Bobby,
followed the coffin to the grave, which he would rarely leave until his own death
fourteen years later. Eventually, a shelter was built in the churchyard for the dog,
and he was fed every day. Bobby's fame spread, many visiting Greyfriars just to see
him. When dog licences were introduced, the ownerless Bobby, of course, had
none, and without a licence would have been put down. However, local citizens
petitioned the Lord Provost, who paid the licence personally; he did not, however, present the terrier with the freedom of Edinburgh, as is often claimed.

Bobby was buried a short distance away from his master in Greyfriars
Churchyard.

⁐▶ *Cross to the west side of Candlemakers Row and turn right, passing Bobby's Bar, to
the adjacent building.*

Location 2   Candlemaker Hall

Candlemaker Row

The hall was built in 1722 for the Society of Candlemakers, and its carved emblem can be seen above a door. In 1654 it was decreed that because of their inflammability it would be safer if candles were manufactured and stored in one street, which is why Candlemaker Row was created. Candles, of course, were the only method of illumination available before gas lighting, and the trade then was extremely important.

➡ *Exit right and continue to Greyfriars Place. First right, enter the gateway to Greyfriars Churchyard.*

Passed immediately left is a prominent 'No dogs' sign, which seems somewhat incongruous as a pink stone ahead commemorates the burial nearby, in unhallowed ground, of Greyfriars Bobby, who was undoubtedly a dog.

➡ *Continue to the east wall of the church, immediately ahead.*

Location 3   Greyfriars Church

Greyfriars Place

❖ Open Easter to October, Monday to Friday 10.30am to 4.30pm, Saturdays 10.30am to 2.30pm; November to March, Thursday 1.30pm to 2.30pm.

In view of its importance in Scottish history and its exceptional location, most visitors to Greyfriars Church are initially disappointed by the unimpressive building that confronts them. Primarily Gothic in appearance due to its pointed windows, the general plainness suggests, correctly, that much has been rebuilt. Fortunately, compensation is offered by the way in which architectural detailing interestingly reflects the complex history of this remarkably accident-prone church.

Greyfriars Church has experienced four major construction periods. The original, post-Reformation church, built 1602–20, was two bays shorter than at present but possessed a west tower, which collapsed in 1718 after gunpowder stored within it had exploded. A separate church, New Greyfriars, was then created to the west, divided from what would be called Old Greyfriars by a party wall; the architect was Alexander McGill. In 1845 fire gutted Old Greyfriars, causing partial collapse of its arcades, the ruins of which were demolished. After the two congregations of Greyfriars had been combined in 1929, Henry F. Kerr remodelled the building, work that was completed just in time to mark the tercentenary of the most important event to take place at Greyfriars: the signing within the building (not its churchyard as depicted in a famous painting) of the National Covenant on 28 February 1638.

Exterior

McGill gave the east gable a pediment in 1722, repeating its obelisk finial on the west gable, and all Greyfriars' buttresses.

➠ *Follow the path ahead, which flanks the north face.*

In addition to destroying the tower, the explosion of 1718 badly damaged the two west bays of the original building, and these were immediately walled off from the rest of the church. McGill restored them and extended the building westward by a further two bays, thus creating two churches of the same dimensions, divided by a shared wall.

The present west end of the church was built by McGill, 1718–21, to complete his two-bay extension to the building. Like the east end, it has a pedimented Dutch gable, but here McGill gave the aisles curvilinear rooflines.

➠ *Enter the north porch.*

Following the damage caused to the two west bays, the north door, which stood in the first of them, was transferred one bay eastward, left, to Old St Giles; it was then given the cherub's-head keystone. In 1721, when creating New St Giles, McGill added another north door in the original position, which is why the nave of St Giles now has twin north doors. McGill added their large porch in 1722.

➠ *Return eastward, enter the church and turn left.*

Interior

Apart from its mid-19th-century lancet windows, the appearance of the east end of Greyfriars Church, formerly Old Greyfriars, reflects Kerr's 1931–38 restoration. He removed the dividing wall and galleries, and replaced the 18th-century plaster ceiling with a timber ceiling above the six most easterly bays of the church, thereby distinguishing the shorter original length of Greyfriars Church, which he emphasised with an arch to the west.

At the south-east corner, the font's carved pedestal, which is said to date from the 1st century, was excavated in Rome.

At the east end of the south wall, an inscribed stone commemorates Margaret, Lady Yester, who died in 1647, aged 75. This was transferred to Greyfriars from Lady Yester's Church in 1938. Burials within churches were forbidden by the Church of Scotland's decree of 1581, which is why, in contrast to England, so few tombs are to be seen in Scottish churches.

Beside the pulpit stands a reproduction of a repentance or cutty (short) stool, on which wrongdoing parishioners, usually erring wives, were forced to sit throughout a service. Offenders also had to endure a scolding from the minister to add to their disgrace.

Mid-19th-century furnishings had replaced those lost within New Greyfriars in the fire of 1845, and their woodwork was re-used by Kerr to create the present organ gallery.

A display at the west end of the church describes the complex history of Greyfriars, which is now the Ecumenical Church of Edinburgh University.

➡ *Exit from Greyfriars and return towards the Greyfriars Place entrance to its churchyard.*

Location 4   Greyfriars Churchyard

In 1562, almost half a century before Greyfriars Church was conceived, Mary, Queen of Scots gave permission for the herb garden of the mendicant Greyfriars, then frugally accommodated at the east end of Grassmarket, to be used as a town graveyard. By this time, the ancient churchyard of St Giles, now entirely lost, had little space left and no expansion was possible.

Facing the entrance from Greyfriars Place, a wooden board has been erected on which the names of famous Edinburghers buried in the churchyard are displayed.

Head for the pink, vertical stone located towards the east end of the church, which marks the burial place of Greyfriars Bobby's master, John Gray.

Greyfriars Churchyard possesses the finest collection of 17th-century monuments in Scotland; most of them, together with later examples of interest, are to be found close to the perimeter wall. Unfortunately, no one appears to be responsible for their upkeep, and the blackened stonework is slowly decaying. As many examples are of great artistic as well as historic value, their neglect seems incomprehensible, particularly in view of the vast amounts of money presently being spent in Edinburgh on public buildings.

Buried in the north-east corner, George Heriot (died 1610), was the founder of the school that bears his name and survives west of the churchyard. Further west, the pedimented Martyr's Monument of 1706, incorporating an open bible, commemorates the Covenanters who had died for their religious beliefs. In the south-west corner William Adam (1689–1748), architect father of the more famous architect brothers, lies in a mausoleum built in 1753 by John Adam; his bust is carved on a panel. Adjacent, a locked gate leads to the Covenanters' Prison.

Following their defeat and capture at the Battle of Bothwell Bridge, more than 1200 Covenanters were held prisoner in an unroofed enclosure within the churchyard for five months, their daily sustenance being one penny loaf each. As the prisoners had to endure the cold of Edinburgh's 1679 winter unprotected from the elements, many perished. Some of their leaders who had survived were deported to work on the Barbados plantations, but their ship sank in a storm off the Scottish coast and more than two hundred drowned.

A coincidentally short distance from the prison, against the south wall, stands the grand Palladian-style mausoleum of the Covenanters' foremost prosecutor, Lord Advocate Sir George Mackenzie, known as 'Bluidy (Bloody) Mackenzie', who died in 1691.

The west gateway from the churchyard punctuates a fragment of Edinburgh's Flodden Wall (see page 84).

➠ *Proceed through this and the next gate ahead to George Heriot's School (only kept unlocked during term time).*

Location 5   George Heriot's School

❖ Occasional open days.

George Heriot, a jeweller and banker to James VI, was known as 'Jinglin' Geordie', apparently because of the large quantity of coins that he always kept on his person. When he died, childless, in 1624, Heriot left a major bequest for establishing a charity school. Although construction began in 1628, its architect, William Wallace, died in 1631 and Cromwell converted the unfinished structure to a military hospital in 1650: in consequence the school was not completed until around 1700.

➠ *Proceed to the north (entrance) facade.*

This facade of the old school has been little altered since it was built, although picturesque cupolas over the corner towers, which soon became unfashionable, had all been dismantled by 1700. Of greatest interest is the elaborate Jacobean centrepiece, which incorporates the main entrance to the school. Reliefs on the frieze above the arch depict goldsmiths (a reference to Heriot's trade), an allegorical Charity, and schoolboys. In a niche above this, Heriot's crest is surmounted by a pediment inscribed with his initials. The dome, with its lantern, was erected above the central tower by Robert Mylne in 1693.

On occasional open days, visitors are permitted to enter the internal courtyard, which is partly arcaded and fitted with stair turrets at each corner. In a wall niche, the figure of Heriot, carved by Robert Mylne, bears a touching Latin inscription, which translates 'My body is represented by this effigy but my soul is represented by this work' (i.e. the charity school). The outer walls of the other three ranges, originally rendered, were given their stone facings in 1833.

➠ *Return eastward through Greyfriars Churchyard to Greyfriars Place. Ahead rises the brand-new, bright pink stone Museum of Scotland. It is entered from the circular tower facing Chambers Street, first right.*

Location 6   Museum of Scotland

Chambers Street

❖ Open Monday to Saturday 10am to 5pm (8pm Tuesday), Sunday 12am to 5pm. ❖ Admission charge (ticket also gives entry to the interconnecting Royal Museum), but free on Tuesday after 4.30pm. ❖ Free guided tours daily at 2.15pm and 3.15pm.

In 1891, the National Museum of Antiquities shared its new building with the National Portrait Gallery, but the space available eventually proved to be inadequate, and for many years the antiquities remained in storage. In December 1998, however, the Museum of Scotland was opened, and all are now on display, housed in a modern building designed by Benson and Forsyth and funded by the National Lottery.

There are seven levels, including a roof terrace with great panoramic views over Edinburgh. It is tempting to take the lift to the fifth floor (a separate lift ascends to the roof terrace) and descend on foot, but exhibits will then be seen in reverse chronological order. Although visitors are given a plan of the museum, the current edition is of little help in locating specific items.

The museum's floor space covers 8,520 sq ft (7,130 sq m) and, unless time is unlimited, a high degree of selectivity is essential. In essence, the basement level 0 deals with geology and the early appearance of Scotland plus its prehistoric people. Look out for a slab of stone from the Roman Antonine Wall (AD 143) and the exquisite Hunterstone Brooch (8th century).

The ground floor, **Kingdom of the Scots 900-1707**, is of greatest interest to most visitors. Here will be found the Monymusk Reliquary, the St Columba Casket and the famous ivory Lewis Chess Pieces. The pieces were carved from walrus tusks in Scandinavia in the 12th century, and discovered in a sand dune on the Isle of Lewis; the museum has fourteen of the set, the remainder being displayed in London's British Museum.

Level 3, **Scotland Transformed 1707-1914**, includes the Jacobite risings: Bonnie Prince Charlie is depicted on a wine glass, and his travelling canteen of cutlery – plus an essential corkscrew – is displayed.

Scottish industry, particularly its 'innovations' is the theme of levels 4 and 5, **Industry and Empire 1707-1914**, while level 6 exhibits 300 20th-century items selected by Scots – Tony Blair unsurprisingly chose an electric guitar.

The Museum of Scotland connects internally at most levels with the adjacent Royal Museum, but some prefer to approach the latter from Chambers Street in order to view its exterior.

➠ *Exit from the museum, right, Chambers Street.*

Location 7   Royal Museum

Chambers Street

❖ Opening times and admission charges as for the Museum of Scotland: see opposite (one ticket gives entry to both museums).

Francis Fowke completed the museum's Italian Renaissance-style building in 1861. Within, delicately balustraded galleries of ironwork overlook the atrium, behind which most of the halls are clustered.

A floor plan (more detailed than the Museum of Scotland's) is available at the reception desk.

The museum is unusually eclectic, just about everything except paintings apparently being eligible for inclusion. However, a great deal of space is given to natural history exhibits, most of which occupy galleries on the east side (left of the entrance), whereas fine arts are kept to the west side; nevertheless, it is still possible, for example, to leave the intricacies of Japanese and Indian sculpture and immediately be confronted with stuffed animals! Although relatively small, the Ancient Egypt collection on the first floor includes some appealing exhibits, including rare examples from the uniquely realistic Armana period.

➠ *Exit to Chambers Street.*

Location 8   Sir William Chambers Monument

Chambers Street

Facing the museum's entrance, this bronze statue of Sir William Chambers, the public health-campaigning Lord Provost after whom the street is named, was erected in 1891. Originally, the town council commissioned a recumbent figure, which its members intended to lie in St Giles Cathedral; this, however, was not permitted by the religious authorities, and the council selected the present site facing the museum. The sculptor, John Rhind, was then briefed to depict Sir William standing in his provost's robes.

➠ *Follow Chambers Street eastward (noting, right, Robert Adam's north facade of Old College). First right South Bridge.*

Location 9   University of Edinburgh Old College

South Bridge

❖ Talbot Rice Gallery open Tuesday to Friday 10am to 5pm, Saturday 10am to 1pm. ❖ Admission free. ❖ Guided tours during the Edinburgh Festival and the Science Festival, Tuesday 1pm to 2pm (at other times individual visitors – but not groups – may visit if convenient).

At the instigation of Edinburgh Town Council, James VI founded the University of Edinburgh by royal charter in 1583. The original college eventually became dilapidated, and when South Bridge was constructed on its east side, 1785–88, profits from leasing the land for it were allocated towards rebuilding it in extended form. Robert Adams was appointed architect and construction began in 1789. Within four years, however, both Adam and the Principal of the University, Adam's cousin William Robertson, were dead and the Napoleonic Wars had begun. Not until 1815, after Napoleon's defeat at Waterloo, did the government give approval for building to recommence. In spite of the addition of many more, widely-spread colleges, Old College (or Old Quad) remains the hub of University activities.

William Playfair, at the age of 27, took over as principal architect, becoming responsible for almost all the interiors and the inner facades of the quadrangle. Externally, however, it is the outer facades of Robert Adam, in particular his entrance range from South Bridge, that are exceptional.

Facing South Bridge, the triple-arched entrance, with monolithic Doric columns, is one of Edinburgh's – and Scotland's – most outstanding architectural features; immediately above, a typically Adam semicircular window adds a magisterial touch.

➠ *Enter the quadrangle.*

Adam intended to bisect the quadrangle with a lateral range, but Playfair preferred a large open space and this was omitted. In the event, all that Adam built within the quadrangle was its north-west quadrant, which Playfair reproduced in the other three corners. Playfair embellished his own impressive north and south elevations with Corinthian pilasters, which convert to columns at the entrances.

Some judge Playfair's west elevation to be insufficiently powerful, but it is not helped by the disproportionately heavy dome that was eventually built over it by Rowand Anderson in 1879. Playfair's east elevation is simply a tame version of Adam's masterpiece on the outer side of the range.

➠ *Enter the Talbot Rice Gallery, where the university's paintings collection is displayed, from the south-west corner of the quadrangle. Other areas are reached via the reception office in the south range.*

In addition to the Talbot Rice Gallery (formerly the Natural History Museum), when not in use visitors may be shown the Playfair Library Hall (formerly the Upper Library Hall), which is Playfair's masterpiece and one of the finest Classical interiors in Britain, and the Elder and Lee Rooms (originally the Senate Rooms). Not by Playfair but usually included in the tour are the Raeburn Rooms - with portraits of three Edinburgh University professors by Raeburn – and the interconnecting Carstares Room. Decor in both dates from the 1880s.

➠ *Exit from Old College to South Bridge. The south, west and north outer facades of Old College, all by Adam, can be admired by proceeding clockwise around them as follows: first right South College Street.*

Although Adam designed the south facade, Playfair unfortunately had to reduce the scale of his centrepiece and pavilions in order to accommodate a larger library than originally planned; the remaining facades are exactly as Adam designed them.

➠ *First right, West College Street, first right Chambers Street (already seen by those who have approached Old College from the Royal Museum). First right, South Bridge continues southward to Nicholson Street where, on its east side, is located Surgeons' Hall.*

Location 10   Surgeons' Hall

Nicholson Street

❖ Museum open by prior arrangement only.

The Ionic temple design of the building, completed in 1832, proclaims this to be the work of William Playfair at his most Grecian. Unusually, and presumably for reasons of economy, the fluted columns are supported by the wall fronting Nicholson Street. Short extensions to the north and south, pedimented like the facade, give the building a T-shaped plan.

Those who have made an appointment may visit the Museum of the Royal College of Surgeons to inspect its collection of medical instruments.

➡ *Return past the Edinburgh University Old College entrance. First right, Infirmary Street. First left, Robertsons Close. Cross to the north side of Cowgate.*

Location 11   Cowgate

As its name suggests, Cowgate marks the route along which cows were once led to pasture. As the area became built up, the street, which runs just south of and parallel with High Street, even exceeding it in length, became a popular area in which to live. Like The Royal Mile, Cowgate remained fashionable until the early 19th century, but by then its wealthy residents had departed, many of them to live in the New Town. Unlike High Street and Canongate, all Cowgate's ancient houses have been demolished, and apart from the Magdalen Chapel at its west end (see page 81) and St Cecilia's Hall ahead, nothing of much architectural interest has survived in this once proud street.

Location 12   St Cecilia's Hall

Cowgate/Niddry Street

In 1763, Robert Mylne designed this concert hall, named to honour the patron saint of music, for the Musical Society of Edinburgh. Now owned by Edinburgh University, its basic use is unchanged, although the hall has been extended and now incorporates a museum. Facing Cowgate, the plain, two-storey building was added in 1812 by the Masonic Grand Lodge, which had bought the property three years earlier.

The foyer, entered from Niddry Street, is screened by Doric columns, and a delicately balustraded staircase ascends to the oval, domed hall, in which chamber concerts and recitals are given.

Housed in the same building is the Russell Collection of ancient harpsichords and clavichords, some of which are played frequently in the concerts.

➟ *Exit and return to Cowgate, left.*

Location 13 Bannerman's
212 Cowgate

Adjacent to the hall, fronting the north side of Cowgate, Bannerman's has miraculously survived as a showpiece Edinburgh tavern. Old benches, scrubbed-pine tables, undecorated stone walls and, a great rarity, a flagstone floor, give the front bar a venerable atmosphere. Bannerman's is very popular with students and live music is often performed.

➟ *Return to St Cecilia's Hall, following Niddry Street to High Street, left. Second right Cockburn Street. Second right Fleshmarket Court. Left Market Street.*

Location 14 City Arts Centre
1-4 Market Street

The ashlar stone, six-storey-plus-attic building was constructed in 1902 as a newsprint store for *The Scotsman* newspaper, located behind it, and later became a fruit warehouse. The City of Edinburgh acquired the building in 1979 and then converted it to become the city's leading municipal art gallery. The core of the permanent collection, which was donated by the Scottish Modern Arts Foundation in 1964, consists primarily of works by Scottish artists from the 17th century to the present. Temporary exhibitions, many of them of them international in stature, are also held in the centre.

Opposite, at No. 29 Market Street, the Fruitmarket Gallery, recently redesigned by Richard Murphy, exhibits work by contemporary artists and architects.

The office of the Edinburgh Military Tattoo occupies Nos 33–34 Market Street. Applications for tickets are accepted by post at the beginning of the year. Performances begin on the first Friday in August and continue throughout the month. Currently the Tattoo proves to be a complete sell-out and early reservations are recommended. Tickets are also sold here for the royal yacht *Britannia*, now docked at Leith (see page 157).

➟ *First right, Waverley Bridge. Direct buses depart from Waverley Bridge to Edinburgh Airport and the* Britannia.

Princes Street

Register House – Sir Walter Scott Monument –
Princes Street – National Gallery of Scotland

This route explores Princes Street and its eastern approaches, all part of the
area covered by the First New Town development, where Edinburgh's
immense Georgian extension began.

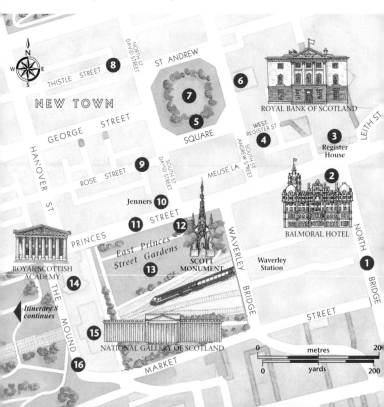

Although some churches, chapels and public buildings were constructed, it was intended that the New Town should be entirely residential: most Edinburghers were expected to cross North Bridge to shop, as before, in the Old Town, and the subsequent popularity of Princes Street as a commercial thoroughfare came as a surprise. In consequence, few unaltered Georgian houses are seen in or around it.

Undoubtedly, the major appeal of this part of the New Town to visitors is its shops, bars and restaurants, plus, of course, the world-famous views of Edinburgh Castle.

Timing: *As very little of this route is under cover, with only three museums and two churches to enter, fine weather is desirable.*

Start:: *The east side of North Bridge, towards its centre.*

Location 1   North Bridge

Before the New Town could be developed, the valley between it and Old Town had to be bridged. However, a major problem was that since the 15th century the narrow, manmade stretch of water known as the Nor' (North) Loch had almost filled the valley, and not until it had been partially drained, 1759–63, could the foundation stone of the North Bridge be laid; due to a series of mishaps it took ten years to build. Widening took place a century later, but when Waverley Station was enlarged, North Bridge had to be entirely rebuilt, the present structure being completed in 1896.

Four stone figures on a plinth supported by stone columns that descend to Waverley Station commemorate the members of the King's Own Borderers Regiment who died in six campaigns, 1878–1902; the memorial was designed by Bernie Rhind in 1906.

➠ *Cross to the west side of the bridge and return southward. First right Princes Street.*

Location 2   Balmoral Hotel

1 Princes Street

The site of the hotel had been virgin land until a development of houses began in 1770. Although it was decreed the following year that no buildings could be erected on the south side of Princes Street between North Bridge and Hanover Street, permission was granted to complete the buildings under construction.

When North Bridge was rebuilt, the houses on the east side of its junction with Princes Street had to be demolished, thereby permitting the development on the site of a large luxury hotel. An architectural competition in 1895 was won by hotel specialist William Hamilton Beattie, who was sent to inspect luxury hotels on the Continent so that the project would be up to date. Naturally, some of the company's committee members had to undertake the onerous task of accompanying him!

The resultant bulky edifice, reminiscent of a Renaissance palace, opened as the North British Station Hotel in 1902. Since its erection, the hotel's clock tower has played an important part in the New Town skyline; incidentally, the time it registers is kept two minutes fast for the benefit of those rushing to catch a train at the adjacent Waverley Station. However, the clock is corrected as midnight approaches on New Year's Eve, so that those celebrating Hogmanay will not be unduly confused.

After complete refurbishment 1988–91, the hotel reopened as The Balmoral. Outstanding salons include the glass-domed Palm Court, and the Sir Walter Scott Grand Ballroom, with its impressive views over Princes Street to the castle.

Surprisingly, Queen Elizabeth, the Queen Mother is listed by the hotel as one of its many distinguished guests. Perhaps her chauffeur was new and misunderstood instructions to make for Balmoral Castle! Some tour operators tell their clients that Sean Connery, who has undoubtedly stayed at the hotel, pays for a suite to be kept permanently available for his use: he does no such thing. Why would a sensible Scot, Edinburgh-born at that, waste money in such a profligate way?

From the west side of the hotel, Waverley Steps descend to Waverley Station, from where visitors are surprised (and if with luggage, somewhat disturbed) to discover that there is no access by lift or escalator to Princes Street. Three stations commissioned by separate railway companies, 1844–47, were rebuilt as one in 1874 and extended as new lines were added. The name Waverley was inspired by Sir Walter Scott's eponymous novel.

Created in 1985 on the site of the former Vegetable Market, and reached directly from Princes Street, the Princes Mall is a covered development of shops and restaurants. On its roof is located the Information Centre of the Edinburgh Tourist Board, which provides a hotel booking service.

On the opposite side of Princes Street, an architectural masterpiece by Robert Adam, Register House, majestically surveys North Bridge.

Opposite: Princes Street and the Balmoral Hotel, with Calton Hill beyond

Location 3   Register House

Princes Street

❖ Open Monday to Friday 10am to 5pm.

A building specifically designed to accommodate Scotland's records was first suggested in 1722, but the foundation stone of Robert Adam's Register House was
not laid until 1774. The City of Edinburgh had donated almost all the site to the
government, hoping that the project would encourage private developers to build
in the New Town.

The facade has not been altered, but due to road widening little remains of its
originally curved forecourt, now known as Wellington Place. Adam designed the
complex as an elongated Palladian villa, but as usual added elegant features to
relieve the austerity of the style. Fluted Corinthian pilasters support the centrepiece and frame the Venetian windows of the end pavilions, which are surmounted by delicate turrets with cupolas. Robert Adam only occasionally visited the site
to supervise construction, entrusting his elder brother John with the task.
Register House was to be the only public building that its architect, who died in
1792, would live to see virtually completed.

➠ *Enter the building and proceed, via the small vestibule, to the rotunda.*

Due to budget restrictions, Adam designed the interiors without undue opulence;
however, his 70 ft (21 m) high rotunda surmounted by a dome never fails to
impress. Most of the interiors of note, however, are by Adam's former student
Robert Reid, who completed the project.

➠ *Exit from the building.*

In front of Register House, the equestrian bronze of the Duke of Wellington was
designed by John Steell in 1848: in consequence it would be known as 'The Iron
Duke in bronze by Steell'! Wellington is depicted riding Copenhagen, his
favourite steed, but the model for it was a horse of similar breed from the Duke
of Buccleuch's stables; its prancing pose is made possible by connecting the tail to
the granite pedestal.

➠ *Follow Princes Street westward. First right West Register Street.*

Location 4   West Register Street

At No. 5, the Guildford Arms is dated 1896 in the glass panel above its entrance.
Internally, the main bar, with its high, Jacobean-style ceiling, can be viewed from
the unusual gallery bar above. Even more unusual in a pub is the revolving door,

which might need careful negotiating after a lengthy session!

➠ *Exit left Gabriel's Road (now just a path). Proceed to the adjacent Café Royal.*

Founded a short distance away from its present site in 1817, the Café Royal transferred here in 1863. Gleaming woodwork within dates from 1901. Outstanding are the rear bar's Doulton ceramic wall tiles depicting seven inventors and two merchant ships; these had been made for Edinburgh's International Exhibition of 1886, and when it closed they were purchased for the tavern. The front bar is reputed to be haunted by a ghost who calls out customers' names behind them, only to disappear as they turn round.

➠ *Exit left. Second right follow St Andrew Street to St Andrew Square and continue to its east range.*

Location 5   St Andrew Square

St Andrew Square, an early part of the first New Town development, is now disappointing as an architectural unit, all its original houses on the south and west sides having been replaced, and on the north side much altered. Fortunately still occupying the centre of the square's east side, Dundas House, now the Royal Bank of Scotland's registered office, is virtually unchanged.

Location 6   Dundas House (Royal Bank of Scotland)

36 St Andrew Square

When Sir Lawrence Dundas, Edinburgh's Member of Parliament, commissioned this mansion from William Chambers in 1771, he expected it to face the church of St Andrew and St George, which was planned to stand in the centre of St Andrew Square, but its location was eventually transferred to George Street. After Dundas died in 1781, the Palladian villa became Scotland's chief Excise Office: the gilded royal coat of arms was added to the pediment, domestic accommodation adapted to offices and extensions were made to the rear. In 1828, after more refurbishment, the building became the head office of the Royal Bank of Scotland. Within, the first-floor boardroom is the only unaltered original apartment; the domed banking hall, one of the finest in Britain, was completed in 1861.

Dressed in a Roman toga, the bronze figure of the 4th Earl of Hopetoun, a former governor of the bank, was erected in front of the building in 1834.

Even though St Andrew Square is no longer residential, as in every other Edinburgh Square (unlike London) the gates to its central garden are kept locked.

Location 7   Melville Monument

This 130 ft (40 m) high copy of Trajan's Column in Rome, originally intended for Calton Hill, was erected in the centre of the garden in 1823 to commemorate the most notable member of the Dundas family, Henry Dundas, 1st Viscount Melville. Due to the extent of his influence, he became known as 'King Henry the Ninth', serving as Treasurer to the Navy 1784–1800, and later First Lord of the Admiralty. Initially no statue of the viscount had been planned to surmount the column, but in 1822 the present figure was commissioned from Sir Francis Chantrey.

➧ *Proceed anticlockwise to the north-west corner of the square. First right North St David Street. First left Thistle Street.*

Location 8   Thistle Street

This street's unpretentious buildings were primarily intended as mews houses for workers and shopkeepers, but wealthier occupants soon joined them, particularly at its east end due to the proximity of fashionable St Andrew Square. The street's name, of course, is a reference to Scotland's national emblem. On the south side, Nos 1 and 2 Thistle Court are believed to have been the first houses built in New Town. Their developer, John Young, who in 1768 also became New Town's first occupant by living in one of them, was awarded £20 from the rates for setting such a good example.

➧ *Return to North St David Street, right, and pass, first right, the intersection with George Street. Second right Rose Street.*

Location 9   Rose Street

In the same way that Thistle Street refers to the national emblem of Scotland, this thoroughfare refers to England's, and celebrates the union of the two countries. Inserted in the road surface at intervals is the Rose emblem, just in case some customers from the street's many bars forget where they are! In 1781 it was decreed that only two-storey houses would be permitted in New Town's minor streets, but as many of Rose Street's houses had already been built three storeys high the regulation here was waived. Pedestrianisation has permitted the street's many bars and restaurants, most of them on the north side, to set chairs and tables outdoors in fine weather, resulting in a lively atmosphere. Originally, all Rose Street's buildings were constructed of stone rubble as houses for 'a better class of artisan' and, as in Thistle Street, a short mews was created behind each block.

At No. 3, the Abbotsford is one of the few survivors from Edinburgh's 'golden age' of pubs, which began in 1880 and ended just before World War I. Competition for business was fierce and labour and materials cheap, resulting in sumptuously carved hardwoods, brass fittings, stained or cut glass, leather upholstery and up-to-date lighting. P.L. Henderson, an architect specialising in pub interiors (he also designed Deacon Brodie's in High Street) was responsible for the Abbotsford, with its stunning island bar of African mahogany.

➠ *Return eastward. First right South St David Street.*

Due to rebuilding, the south sectors of the short thoroughfares that cross George Street retain less of their original Georgian appearance than their north sectors.

Ahead, the view incorporates the spikily romantic but blackened Scott Monument, in East Princes Street Gardens. The Princes Street corner block on the west side, right, is occupied by Scotland's leading department store.

➠ *Right Princes Street.*

Location 10   Jenners

48 Princes Street

When founded, Jenners store was accommodated in former residential houses on Princes Street, but these burned down in 1892 and were replaced by a five-storey-plus-attic structure designed by W. Hamilton Beattie, at the time one of the largest shops in Europe, which has gradually been extended. Faced in pink stone and designed with Renaissance features, Jenners externally retains a pleasingly old-fashioned atmosphere, which is matched within the store.

➠ *Cross to the south side of Princes Street.*

Location 11   Princes Street

Although few of its shops are of outstanding interest, and its architecture has degenerated to a mishmash of styles, Princes Street remains one of the world's great thoroughfares, and is a must on every visitor's agenda. The reason, of course, is the uninterrupted series of views towards Edinburgh Castle, perched dramatically on its escarpment, which can be admired continuously from the street once the Balmoral Hotel has been passed.

Called St Giles Street on Craig's original plan, Princes Street was eventually named to honour, collectively, the sons of George III. Surprisingly, the street's popularity was not predicted, and no houses were ever built on it that could compare in grandeur with the finest in Queen Street or George Street, let alone the New Town's two squares. In spite of early commercialization, some original Georgian houses have survived, mostly at the west end, although virtually all of these have been drastically altered, particularly at ground-floor (shop front) level.

It is strongly recommended that the initial promenade along Princes Street and its gardens is made from east to west so that the castle is always kept in view. If the weather is fine a reasonably early start is preferable because then the east flanks of the Old Town buildings, including the castle, will be dramatically illuminated by the sun – assuming that it shines. From the south side, the gardens provide a more attractive frame to the views than the busy road. Forays across Princes Street to visit selected shops will not be particularly hazardous.

➧ *Enter East Princes Street Gardens and proceed towards the Sir Walter Scott Monument.*

Location 12   Sir Walter Scott Monument

Princes Street

❖ Open March to May and October, Monday to Saturday 9am to 6pm, Sunday 10am to 6pm; June to September, Monday to Saturday 9am to 8pm, Sunday 10am to 6pm; November to February, Monday to Saturday 9am to 4pm, Sunday 10am to 4pm. ❖ Admission charge.

Funds for a monument to Scotland's greatest romantic novelist, Sir Walter Scott, who died in 1832, were donated by members of the public, and a competition to design it in the Gothic style attracted 55 entrants, many of whom were renowned sculptors. In third place came George Meikle Kemp, an unknown carpenter and self-taught architect; however, after further drawings had been submitted and judged, it was his scheme that was eventually chosen. As on other occasions in the New Town, the monument was originally intended to stand elsewhere, in this case Charlotte Square, but it was eventually decided that the present site was more suitable. Unfortunately, Kemp would never see his masterpiece completed.

It was the designer's habit to walk home to his wife and family every evening along the banks of the Union Canal, but one evening in 1844 he did not return, and his body was found floating in the canal. Whether he had slipped, taken a dram too many, committed suicide or been pushed over the bank was never discovered. Although by now funds for the monument had been used up, it proved an easy task to raise more, and Kemp's brother-in-law, William Bonnar, completed the work.

John Steell's seated figure of Scott (Kemp had wanted an upright pose) with his deerhound Maida beside him was installed on its platform in 1846; it was the first statue of marble to be erected in Edinburgh. Various artists carved the 64 statues of characters from Scott's novels that occupy the niches in the structure; a further 16 statuettes represent Scottish poets.

➠ *Enter the monument by its south door.*

From the upper gallery, approached by 287 steps, some of the finest views in the city can be gained. On the way up, the first gallery, located directly above the great arches, leads to a Museum Room, created in 1855 from an open area.

Although recently restored, the monument was not cleaned, apparently for fear of losing its detail. This seems a great pity, as the natural colour of the monument's different sandstones is a delightful pale gold rather than sooty grey merging to coal-black as at present. However, the successful recent cleaning of Grande Place in Brussels by laser gives hope for the future.

➠ *Exit from the monument left.*

Sir Walter Scott Monument

Location 13   East Princes Street Gardens

Princes Street

❖ Closed at dusk.

Earth excavated for the construction of New Town's buildings was used to fill the drained Nor'Loch, and in 1830 owners of the Princes Street properties paid for the area to be laid out and planted as their private gardens; they paid £1 for a key to the gate, but in a short time anyone could obtain a duplicate and the gardens were eventually opened to the public.

When Waverley Station was enlarged in 1892, part of it intruded on the gardens, unfortunately, a proposal to cover the structure's roof with turf was never put into effect.

Bronze memorials proliferate in the gardens as follows: east of the Scott Monument, David Livingstone (1876), doctor, explorer and missionary, who, believed lost in Africa, achieved immortality when the American H.M. Stanley discovered him; west of the Scott Memorial, Adam Black (1877), founder of publishers A&C Black, a Lord Provost and a Liberal MP; further west Professor John Wilson (1865).

➠ *Follow Princes Street westward, remaining on its south side.*

Nos 64–69, now BHS, completed in 1965, was the first building to comply with the regulation that all new structures in Princes Street should incorporate a first-floor balcony as part of a proposed street-long upper-level walkway. The scheme failed, much less rebuilding taking place than expected.

Two adjacent Grecian-style buildings erected on The Mound ahead indicate the hand of William Playfair.

Location 14   Royal Scottish Academy

The Mound

❖ Open Monday to Saturday 10am to 5pm (during the Festival 10am to 6pm), Sunday 2pm to 5pm (during the Festival 11am to 6pm). ❖ Admission charge.

The building was completed in 1826 as the Royal Institution, to accommodate the Royal Society, the Society of Antiquities and the Institute for the Encouragement of the Fine Arts. Five years later, William Playfair was asked to enlarge his Greek Doric 'temple' to cope with the expansion of these three august bodies. He almost doubled the length by extending it southward by seven bays. At the same time he added decorative features and advanced the portico towards the road by an additional row of columns. In 1844 the statue of the young Queen Victoria as Britannia was installed overlooking Princes Street.

All the original occupants of the building had moved elsewhere by 1909, and it was then remodelled internally for the Royal Scottish Academy. Major exhibitions are held during the Festival, and the Academy's Annual Exhibition takes place from March to July; throughout the rest of the year, works by Scottish art societies are exhibited.

➠ *Proceed south of the Academy to the National Gallery of Scotland.*

Location 15   National Gallery of Scotland

The Mound

❖ Opening times as for the Royal Scottish Academy: see opposite. ❖ Admission free for the permanent collection. An admission charge is levied for special exhibitions during the Festival.

The foundation stone of Playfair's National Gallery was laid by Prince Albert in 1850, 24 years after the building now occupied by the Royal Scottish Academy had been completed. Until 1909 the premises were shared with the latter, double porticos at both ends and single porticos on each side providing separate entrances. The gallery's building has fewer decorative features than the academy's, indicative of a more restricted budget.

Princes Street and The Mound

The Collection

Although, as may be expected, Scottish painters are prominent, works by the Impressionists and Postimpressionists are outstanding, and the collection of Old Masters is only surpassed in Britain by that of London's National Gallery.

The collection includes the following highlights:

Main Floor: Rembrandt, *Self-portrait*; Turner, Views of Rome; Constable, *Vale of Dedham*; Gainsborough, *The Hon. Mrs Graham*; Sargent, *Lady Agnew of Lochnair*; Vermeer, *Christ in the House of Martha and Mary* (the painter's largest and earliest-known work); Rubens, *Feast of Herod.*

Lower Floor: Raeburn, *The Rev. Robert Walker Skating on Duddingston Loch*; Nasmyth, *Princes Street 1825*; Sir William Allen, *The Murder of Rizzio.*

Upper Floor (rear sector): Paintings by Renoir, Monet, Degas, Gauguin, Van Gogh and Cézanne.

Upper Floor (front sector, reached by short staircase facing the entrance): Raphael, *Bridgwater Madonna, Holy Family with Palm Trees, Madonna del Passeggio*; Hugo van der Goes (?) *Trinity Panels.*

Trinity Panels

The Trinity Panels, on permanent loan from HM The Queen, are the only significant religious works of art predating the Reformation to have survived in Scotland. Those who have visited the Brass Rubbing Centre in the former Church of Trinity College (see page 54) will have seen the building for which these painted panels were commissioned in the mid-15th century, probably as wings of a triptych altarpiece, but possibly as organ shutters; the work is attributed to Hugo van der Goes. To permit visitors to view both sides, staff turn the panels every half hour.

The fronts of the panels portray, left, James III beside St Andrew (who bears his cross); the youth behind the king may be his son, the future James IV. On the right, James's consort, Margaret of Denmark, is kneeling in front of St Canute, patron saint of Denmark, who wears armour.

The reverse panels depict, left, the Holy Trinity and right, kneeling, Sir Edward Bonkil, the first provost of Trinity College, accompanied by two angels. Obviously, the missing central panel must have depicted the object of veneration, possibly a Virgin and Child painting, but there is no record of this.

➠ *Exit and proceed to the south-east corner of the building, from where Playfair Steps climb steeply to Old Town.*

This flight was named to commemorate William Playfair, the architect of the two art galleries passed. During the Festival the approach to the steps is lined with stalls from which all kinds of souvenirs are sold, buskers perform and a lively atmosphere prevails.

➠ *Return to Princes Street, left. First left The Mound.*

Location 16   The Mound

Almost marking Princes Street's halfway point, The Mound runs southward, sub-dividing the East and West Princes Street gardens, and skirting the west side of the Royal Scottish Academy and the National Gallery of Scotland. Its route was made possible by the creation of a causeway known as The Mound, which comprised 1,305,780 cartloads of earth and rubble excavated for the first New Town development. Begun in 1781 by George Boyd, a Lawnmarket clothier, to provide access for the convenience of his New Town clients, The Mound was referred to as 'Geordie Boyd's Mud Brig'. Initially it bisected the soggy remnants of the Nor'Loch, the drainage of which had begun in 1759. At last, in 1835, the 50-year-old Mound, by then a muddy eyesore, was landscaped and its road laid out; ironically, it appears that what had been George Boyd's shop in Old Town had to be demolished for it.

➠ *Enter West Princes Street Gardens through the gateway west of The Mound.*

Location 17   West Princes Street Gardens

| Princes Street |

❖ Closed at dusk.

Of much greater extent than East Princes Street Gardens, these gardens originally covered even more land than they do now, winding around Castle Rock to its south side until the 1820s, when new roads were laid out. Residents of Princes Street leased the gardens from the local authority for their private use in 1816, but 60 years later they were reacquired and opened to the public.

Although not specifically prohibited, no permission had ever been given to build on the south side of Princes Street west of Hanover Street, and in 1816 an Act of Parliament forbade it in perpetuity. The gardens are beautifully maintained, and the railway track, laid in its cutting in 1846, is barely noticeable. Monuments proliferate, most of them military and cast in brass.

Laid out just within the north-east entrance to the gardens, Edinburgh's Floral Clock, the first of the genre, is replanted each spring. The mechanism of the clock and its model cuckoo, which announces each hour, is operated from within the plinth of the adjacent statue.

Allan Ramsay (1686–1758), the poet and father of the painter of the same name, is commemorated by the white Carrara marble statue that faces Princes Street immediately west of the Floral Clock. Lord Murray, a descendant of Ramsay, commissioned the statue, which was erected here in 1865. The four medallions on its plinth depict Ramsay's wife, two of his great-granddaughters, General Ramsay (grandson of the poet), and Lord Murray.

➠ *Follow the path that returns eastward, descending to the cottage below.*

Robert Morham, who rearranged the gardens in the late 19th century, lived in the red sandstone cottage.

➠ *Past the cottage descend the steps, left.*

Designed in a wide semicircle, the Royal Scots Memorial, the largest of the gardens' monuments, commemorates the battles fought by the oldest regiment in Britain – from Tangiers (1680) to Burma (1943–45). Between the stone slabs, bronze medallion heads represent all Scotland's rulers from Charles I to George VI – including Oliver Cromwell.

➠ *Follow the main path westward.*

To the left, a charming group of allegorical figures by William Brodie represents *The Genius of Architecture Crowning the Theory and Practise of Art*.

➠ *Continue ahead to the open-air theatre and follow the path, right, to Princes Street, right. Alternatively, ascend the grassy mound – it is quicker.*

From the gardens, the Royal Scots Greys Monument overlooks Princes Street at the junction with Frederick Street. Its equestrian bronze of a Royal Scots Grey Trooper was designed by Birnie Rhind in 1906. Plaques commemorate members of the regiment killed in the Boer War (Princes Street side), and both World Wars (gardens side).

➠ *Remaining within the gardens, turn right and follow the upper path westward.*

The Scottish-American War Memorial, installed in 1927, is a tribute from US citizens of Scottish descent to Scots who fought in World War I. It was designed by R. Tait Mackenzie of Philadelphia, who used several models for the kilted young soldier earnestly gazing heavenward apparently in search of divine approval. The plinth is simply inscribed 'The Call'. A bronze relief curves behind the figure, illustrating the many and varied occupations that Scottish volunteers had to vacate in order to fight for their country.

➠ *Continue westward and turn right, ascending to Princes Street.*

Facing the Castle Street junction, the Portland stone figure, erected in 1910, depicts Dr Thomas Guthrie, bible in hand, taking a poor boy into his care. Guthrie, a philanthropist, founded the Ragged Schools.

➠ *Descend towards the rear of the open-air theatre. First right cross the railway line and follow the narrow upper path that continues westward following the base of Castle Hill. On the left is a ruined tower.*

Location 18   Wellhouse Tower

The tower was built in 1326 to defend Edinburgh Castle's freshwater well and its western entrance. Two of its storeys have survived on three sides; windows facing Castle Rock overlook a narrow passage, which originally could be blocked by a gate. No trace of a well now exists, but it is believed to have been sunk below the square projection dating from the 17th century at the tower's north-east corner. Directly above the tower, a flat stone slab known as the Crane Seat served as a base from which aggressors below could be bombarded.

➠ *Descend (a bit of a scramble) by the narrow path from the tower's entrance to the main path below. Further west a bridge, right, crosses the railway line. Ahead stands a remarkable fountain.*

Location 19   Ross Fountain

This French Second Empire cast-iron fountain was produced in Paris for Edinburgh's International Exhibition of 1862. When it ended, the fountain was purchased by gunsmith Daniel Ross, who presented it to Edinburgh. Dean Ramsay pronounced its buxom maidens and brash design 'grossly indecent, disgusting, insulting, offensive and disgraceful' – it seems he didn't like it.

➠ *Follow the path westward and enter the gateway of St Cuthbert Church. Continue through its graveyard towards the south-west entrance.*

Location 20   St Cuthbert

Lothian Road

❖ Open Sunday to Friday; also Saturday, April to September.

By tradition, St Cuthbert, Bishop of Lindisfarne, personally founded a church on this site in the 7th century. However, a St Cuthbert Church is not recorded in Edinburgh until 1127; it is known that six buildings have been constructed on the site since then. A spire was added to the medieval structure in 1790, but a century later the body of the church was found to be unsafe, and in 1894 its replacement, designed by Hippolyte Blanc, was dedicated. All that he retained externally from the former building was its Georgian steeple.

➠ *Enter the vestibule.*

Immediately right, a wall plaque from the former building commemorating the Redfern children was carved by John Flaxman. Another plaque on the same wall commemorates John Napier (Joannis Neperi), the inventor of logarithms, who was buried at St Cuthbert in 1617. Made in 1842, the title page of Napier's book is represented.

➠ *Enter the nave.*

In 1922, the nave was reduced in length to provide more space at the west end of the church. Blanc was responsible for designing the stalls, pulpit and organ cases.

The apse is adorned with an impressive Arts and Crafts frieze of alabaster, installed in 1908. Its design is based on Leonardo da Vinci's painting of *The Last Supper*.

➠ *Leave St Cuthbert by its west exit and proceed ahead to Lothian Road, remaining on its east side. Immediately opposite stands the Caledonian Hotel.*

The Renaissance-style Caledonian Hotel was built in 1903 of red sandstone. Like the Balmoral Hotel, it was originally a station hotel. The completely new block to the rear was added in 1971.

➠ *Continue ahead towards the Princes Street junction.*

Location 21   St John

Lothian Road/Princes Street

❖ Open Sunday to Friday, also Saturday, April to September.

One of Edinburgh's finest examples of Gothic Revival architecture, St John was designed by William Burn and completed in 1818. During the Festival its grounds are almost entirely occupied by a Crafts Market.

Internally, the nave's soaring arches and fan vaults, although of plaster, are convincingly 'Perpendicular Gothic'. The chancel was extended by one bay and given its apse in 1882. At the east end of the north aisle, the marble bust of Dean Stanley is by John Steell.

➠ *Exit from the church right. First right Princes Street. Remain on the south side.*

On the north side of Princes Street the facades of Nos 142-44, both early buildings, appear as though they are being devoured by the curtain walling 'dentures' constructed around them by Basil Spence for the Royal Bank of Scotland in 1976: a more risible example of 'conservation' is difficult to imagine.

Further east, in the same block, Macdonalds occupies the ground floor of original Princes Street buildings, which refreshingly have kept their glazing bars to the windows on the floors above.

In the block to the east of the South Charlotte Street intersection, Waterstone's bookshop (No. 128) boasts a dramatic double-bow window, which, although it appears to be Georgian, dates from 1866, when the building was commissioned by the University Club.

➠ *Itinerary 9 continues from this point.*

George Street

Charlotte Square – The Georgian House – George Street –
Scottish National Portrait Gallery

Following on from Itinerary 8, this route returns eastward through New Town, exploring elegant George Street and its side streets. A highlight is the lively central sector of Rose Street – Edinburgh's Soho.

Timing: *The Georgian House and the Scottish National Portrait Gallery are the only museums on this itinerary, and fine weather is therefore desirable. Some may wish to take the bus from Charlotte Square to the Scottish National Gallery of Modern Art and the neighbouring Dean Gallery (Itinerary 11).*

Start: *The west end of Princes Street at its junction with South Charlotte Street.*

Alexander Graham Bell (1847–1922) was born at 14 South Charlotte Street, as commemorated by the stone plaque beside the door. Bell eventually emigrated to the USA, where, at Boston in 1875, he invented the telephone.

➡ *Continue northward to Charlotte Square, first right.*

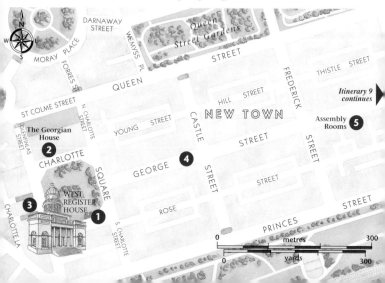

Location 1 Charlotte Square

This square, the final stage in the first part of the New Town development, is undoubtedly its showpiece. In no other New Town thoroughfare were the facades of every house designed by one architect. Robert Adam presented his proposals in 1791, a year before his death, and the first house was roofed by 1795. However, in spite of this initially speedy progress, Charlotte Square was not completed until 1820. St George Square, the name originally chosen for it, was eventually changed to please Charlotte, George III's consort.

Least altered from Adam's original scheme is the north range ahead, where the square's anticlockwise numbering begins. Although Adam specified statues and a decorative frieze to each centrepiece, they were never executed. However, as can be seen, his wish that sphinxes should embellish the end pavilions was respected, but only on this range. Until 1999 No. 6 was the Secretary of State for Scotland's official residence, but it is now assigned to Scotland's First Minister.

➠ *Enter the adjoining house.*

Location 2 The Georgian House

7 Charlotte Square

❖ Open April to October, Monday to Saturday 10am to 5pm, Sunday 2pm to 5pm. ❖ Admission charge.

Although Adam designed the exterior of this house, its interior, as was usual in New Town, is the work of another architect: in this instance Edmund Butterworth, who, in 1796, designed the accommodation for John Lamont. The house has been decorated and furnished in the late 18th-century manner by the National Trust for Scotland, which owns the property.

Flagstones in the hallway are much restored, but the original cornices have survived. Although all but one of the chimneypieces in the house are contemporary, none was made for it. As demonstrated, it was usual for the main bedchamber to be located on the ground floor overlooking the garden – and also a convenient stagger away from the dining room!

➠ *Ascend to the first floor.*

Overlooking the square, the Drawing Room is the grandest room in the house. To its rear, the Parlour would be used frequently as an informal, dining room.

The kitchen, in the basement, was painted blue as there was a belief that flies disliked this colour; the range and sink are not original but the stone compartments within the adjacent wine cellar are unaltered.

➠ *Exit right and proceed to the west range of the square.*

Location 3 West Register House

Charlotte Square

In 1791, Adam designed the church of St George as the centrepiece of the square's west range. However, as part of the economies that had to be made, Robert Reid, his successor, completely redesigned the dome to resemble a sleek version of that of St Paul's Cathedral in London.

St George opened in 1814 and remained the parish church until 1961 when, having become structurally unsafe, it was closed. Renovation as a church would have been too expensive, and in 1965 the building was converted to a branch of the Scottish Record Office, reopening as West Register House in 1971. Public exhibitions are held in the foyer.

The square's central garden was enlarged to accommodate the bronze equestrian memorial to Prince Albert, unveiled in 1876. John Steell, who designed it, was knighted during the ceremony.

Bus 13 departs from the south-west corner of the square to the National Gallery of Modern Art, the Dean Gallery and the Water of Leith (Itinerary 11). The same bus also stops in George Street between Castle Street and Frederick Street, and in Frederick Street at its junction with Hill Street.

➠ *From the north-east corner of Charlotte Square, follow Charlotte Street northward. First right, Young Street. Remain on the south side.*

At No. 43, The Oxford Bar, Edinburgh's most intimate pub, has a very narrow ground-floor bar, from which steps lead to the somewhat larger saloon. Very much a regular's watering hole, strangers are nevertheless made welcome.

➠ *Exit right. First right, Castle Street.*

North of its George Street intersection, many of Castle Street's houses are bow-fronted and little altered. No 39 was occupied by Sir Walter Scott, 1802–26.

Location 4 George Street

As George Street follows the crest of the ridge on which the first New Town development was built, it was always intended to be the main artery of the quarter; eventually, however, Princes Street became far more important. Each of George Street's three central intersections are embellished with statues and provide cameo views of the distant Firth of Forth to the north and Old Town to the south.

At the North Castle Street junction, the bronze figure commemorates Thomas Chalmers (1780–1847), social reformer and first Moderator of the Free Church of Scotland. John Steell modelled the figure in 1847, although it was not erected until 1878.

➡ *Proceed eastward.*

Probably the best example of an original George Street house is the simple but elegant No. 91. Two doors further on, at No. 87, the late-Georgian shop interior of Hamilton & Inches was fitted in 1835.

At the Frederick Street intersection (first left), Chantrey's bronze statue of William Pitt was erected in 1833.

➡ *Follow Frederick Street northward.*

The street's name commemorates Frederick, Prince of Wales, father of George III, who was killed by a cricket ball.

No. 43, Café Rouge, retains Ionic pilasters on its frontage.

➡ *Return southward and pass the George Street intersection. First right Rose Street.*

The pedestrianisation of Rose Street began at this sector in 1968, thereby encouraging the proliferation of bars and restaurants that has made the street Edinburgh's 'Soho'. As long as it is reasonably warm and dry, tables and chairs miraculously appear on the former sidewalks.

On the south side, at Nos 152–4, The Kenilworth Bar was created in 1904 by remodelling the two lower storeys of a late 18th-century house. A high, Jacobean-style ceiling, impressive brass chandeliers, ceramic tiles up to clerestory level and venerable woodwork make this one of Edinburgh's outstanding pub interiors.

➡ *Return eastward, pass the Frederick Street junction, cross to the north side and proceed towards the end of the block.*

The Rose Street Brewery, at Nos 55–57 Rose Street, brews its 70 and 80 shilling Auld Reekie ale on the first floor, as can be observed from the adjacent Brewhouse Lounge.

⮕ *Return westward. First right Frederick Street. First right George Street.*

On the south side, The Standing Order, at Nos 62–66, is a pub tastefully converted for Wetherspoon in 1997 from a Bank of Scotland branch designed by David Bryce in 1874. The main bar and restaurant occupy the former telling room, the ornate ceiling of which has been retained.

⮕ *Exit to George Street, right (there is also a rear exit to Rose Street).*

Location 5 Assembly Rooms

54 George Street

The Assembly Rooms, originally a venue for ballroom dancing, now serves as a major venue for Festival Fringe events. John Henderson designed this pilastered Roman Doric building, which opened in 1787. From the outset it was regarded as excessively austere – even for Edinburgh – and Robert Adam suggested a scheme to enliven its facade; nothing was done, however, until 1818, when the Doric portico overlooking George Street was added by William Burn. Almost 50 years later, the first-floor ballroom was extended into the centre of the portico, rather spoiling its appearance. The lower, arched extremities on both sides of the building were added in 1907. Within, the ballroom's Corinthian pilasters and chandeliers date from 1796.

⮕ *Exit right and continue eastward.*

Trotters, at No. 44, attracts the many visitors who just come to admire this optician's late-Georgian shop front, the finest in Edinburgh.

⮕ *Continue eastward to the Hanover Street junction.*

From this point, the view southward embraces a famously varied combination of Edinburgh architecture. In the foreground are Playfair's 'Grecian temples', behind which the medieval closes of Old Town wind upward towards the slender spires of its Victorian churches.

⮕ *From the centre of the George Street/Hanover Street intersection rises the statue of George IV.*

Location 6 George IV Statue

George Street

Even though the statue of George IV, by Chantrey, was not erected until 1831, it commemorates the king's visit to Edinburgh in 1822, the first by a British monarch to Scotland since the Battle of Culloden in 1746. In spite of outrageous profligacy and philandering, George IV, who died in 1830, remained popular in Scotland.

➡ *Continue eastward and cross to the south side of George Street.*

Location 7   The Dome

14 George Street

This is Edinburgh's most spectacular example of converting a bank into a restaurant, work that was completed in 1993. The building was constructed for the Commercial Bank of Scotland in 1847 by David Rhind, who may have based his classical design on Playfair's Surgeons' Hall. The pediment of the enormous Corinthian portico is embellished with a bas-relief, by James Wyatt, of Caledonia flanked by allegorical figures. The enormous grill room, the restaurant's centre-piece, occupies the original telling hall, the domed ceiling of which has given the restaurant its name.

➡ *Exit and cross to the south side of George Street.*

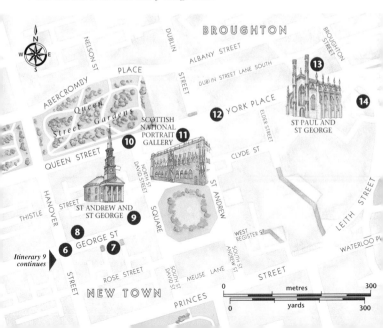

Location 8   George Inter-Continental Hotel

19–21 George Street

Visitors enter the hotel at the double-fronted No 21, but Nos 15, 17 and 19, together with a modern extension to the rear, also form part of the complex. Three separate properties, Nos 15 to 19, built by Robert Young around 1782, were combined in 1879 to provide a hotel. Many alterations have since taken place, but at no stage was Robert Adam involved, in spite of misleading suggestions to the contrary. The complex opened in 1950 as the George Hotel.

▥▶ *Continue eastward to the centre of the same block.*

Location 9   St Andrew and St George

George Street

Originally intended to occupy the centre of St Andrew Square, the church, designed by Major Andrew Frazer, was built here instead. Inconveniently, this end of George Street had already been built up, and some new houses had to be demolished in order to make space for the church, which was originally called St Andrew (St George, now West Register House, already having been planned for Charlotte Square). Its oval plan was the first British example of importance.

The body of the church was completed in 1784, but its steeple, designed by Alex Stevens, was not finished until three years later. Internally, the ceiling is Adamesque and original pews survive in the gallery.

▥▶ *Exit left and continue eastward. First right follow St Andrew Square to North St David Street. First left Queen Street.*

Location 10   Queen Street

Queen Street stretches westward, providing Edinburgh's most impressive sequence of little-altered Georgian houses. Development was only permitted on the south side, as the open views over Queen Street Gardens to the Firth of Forth were from the start regarded as inviolate (unlike the views of Old Town from Princes Street). Fortunately, commercialisation has had little effect on the street's appearance, most owners of the New Town's shops, hotels and offices preferring to be located close to the 'action' between George Street and Princes Street.

▥▶ *Continue a short distance westward and cross to the north side of Queen Street, from where the exteriors of Nos 8 to 10 (on the south side) may best be appreciated.*

Robert Adam designed No. 8 for Baron Orde, a house that Boswell described as 'elegant'; its mansard roof is original and the frontage unusually wide.

Having sold their existing hall, the Royal College of Physicians of Edinburgh purchased an existing house, which they replaced in 1844 with the present delightfully neo-classical Nos 9–10. Its architect, Thomas Hamilton, was inspired by the Tower-of-the-Winds and surmounted the portico and pediment with statues of Greek physicians. Nos 8-10 were united internally in 1957.

⟶ *Return eastward along Queen Street, pass the North St David Street junction, and cross to the north side of Queen Street.*

Location 11 Scottish National Portrait Gallery

Queen Street

❖ Open Monday to Saturday 10am to 5pm, Sunday 2pm to 5pm (11am to 5pm during the Festival). ❖ Admission free (except for some special exhibitions).

Architect Rowand Anderson planned this building to be shared originally by the Gallery and the Antiquities Museum (now accommodated in the new Museum of Scotland). Opened in 1890, the Gothic design of its red sandstone exterior was influenced in part by that of the Doge's Palace in Venice. Canopied niches shelter statues by various sculptors. Within, the frieze of the Great Hall depicts scenes from Scottish history. The ground floor is reserved for special exhibitions.

Only one-third of the collection can be shown at any one time, and even the highlights, particularly modern works, are 'rested' on occasions.

⟶ *Ascend by a lift to the second floor.*

Many find the first gallery, The Age of Burns and Scott, the most interesting. A portrait of Sir Walter Scott, by Raeburn is exhibited on the wall facing the entrance. On the wall right, the painting of the Earl of Seaforth in Naples, by Pietro Fabris, is of particular interest as the 14-year-old boy playing the clavier in the background has recently been identified as Mozart. Also in the painting is Sir William Hamilton, the British envoy to Naples, whose wife Emma became the mistress of Nelson.

Usually displayed on the entrance wall is the only known contemporary likeness of the poet Robert Burns, painted by his friend Alexander Nasmyth in 1787.

The next gallery, From Independence to Union, exhibits paintings of royalty. On either side of the entrance are portraits of Mary of Guise and her daughter Mary, Queen of Scots, but neither are contemporary. Lord Darnley, aged nine, appears to have been a striking looking boy. On the end wall is Bonnie Prince Charlie, aged 12, and his father, the Old Pretender, aged three. The painter Weesop was an eyewitness of the execution of Charles I in London's Whitehall, and his gory depiction of the regicide is a highlight of the collection.

➡ *Descend by lift to the first floor's Twentieth-Century galleries.*

Exhibits may include: Kokoschka's 1969 painting of the 14th Duke of Hamilton and his wife (who were surprisingly visited by Hitler's deputy, Rudolf Hess, in 1941), Jo Grimond, by Patrick Heron, Ludovic Kennedy and his wife, the former ballet dancer Norma Shearer, and the Queen Mother, a delicate painting commissioned by the gallery from Avigdor Arikha.

➡ *Descend to the ground floor, exit left and proceed eastward to the Dublin Street (first left) intersection.*

From this end of Dublin Street can be gained one of Edinburgh's finest views northward over the Firth of Forth.

➡ *Continue eastward to York Place. Remain on the south side.*

Location 12   York Place

York Place was originally identified as a continuation of Queen Street, although nothing was constructed until 1793.

On the north side, most of Nos 2–40 retain their original fanlights but all the dormer windows are later additions.

At No 32, Raeburn House, Sir Henry Raeburn painted and exhibited his work from 1798 to 1809.

➡ *Continue eastward to the end of York Place, remaining on the north side.*

Location 13   St Paul and St George

York Place

Built by Archibald Elliot in 1818, this church was originally dedicated only to St Paul, gaining its second dedication when the congregation amalgamated with that of the Episcopal Church of St George, formerly located at No. 5 York Place. The external Gothic Perpendicular detailing is refreshing in its accuracy and lightness of touch.

Internally, late 19th-century alterations and an east extension resulted in a much more spacious interior. Brought from St George's Episcopal Church was Sir Walter Scott's box pew and the late 18th-century font.

➠ *Exit left, first right Broughton Street.*

Location 14 St Mary's Cathedral

Broughton Street

A Catholic chapel designed by James Graham in 1813 forms the core of St Mary's, which was granted cathedral status (RC) in 1878. The nave was rebuilt, with aisles and a clerestory, in 1891, followed by a new chancel in 1895. In 1932 the low nave was heightened and given a second clerestory; its roof is supported internally by enormous wooden angels designed in the stylistic manner of the period.

➠ *Exit from the cathedral to Broughton Street.*

Outside the cathedral the three enormous bronzes are the work of Sir Eduardo Paolozzi, Her Majesty's Sculptor in Ordinary in Scotland, who was born at Leith. Inscribed on a giant foot, a Latin quotation reflects the links between Scotland and Italy.

➠ *Return northward along Broughton Street. First right Picardy Place.*

Picardy Place, built 1803–09, was named to commemorate a colony of French Protestant silk-weavers who had emigrated to the area from Picardy in the 17th century to escape Louis XIV's religious intolerance. Demolition in 1969 for road improvements resulted in the loss of the street's south side, which included No. 11, the birthplace of Sir Arthur Conan Doyle. Approximately marking its location is a bronze figure depicting Sherlock Holmes, the work of Gerald Ogilvie Laing, 1991.

➠ *Continue eastward to Leith Walk and cross immediately to its east side.*

The Playhouse Theatre was built as Edinburgh's largest cinema in 1929, but remodelled in 1980. It currently specializes in London West End musicals performed by touring companies.

➠ *Return southward to Leith Walk's junction with Princes Street and Waterloo Place (Itinerary 10).*

Holyrood and Calton Hill

Calton Hill – The Palace of Holyroodhouse –
Dynamic Earth – Parliament Buildings

Although the obvious approach to Holyrood is from Canongate (Itinerary 5), in fine weather a more scenic and quicker route from Princes Street is via Calton Hill, which most will wish to visit in any case.

Timing: *Coach parties begin to arrive at the summit of Calton Hill around 9.30am, and those wishing to experience the hill at its most tranquil are advised to make an early start.*

Start: *The east end of Princes Street. Proceed eastward.*

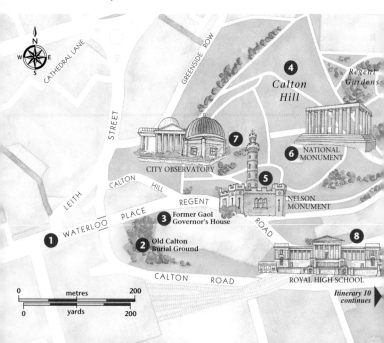

Location 1   Waterloo Place

Archibald Elliot designed this east extension to Princes Street in 1815, the year of the decisive Battle of Waterloo – hence its name. Waterloo Place was designed as four palatial blocks, and little else has occurred to alter them; only when the middle section is reached does it become apparent that a bridge had to be constructed over the Calton ravine. At this point, Ionic screens are inscribed: on the north side 'The Regent's Bridge commenced in the ever memorable year 1815', and on the south side 'Opened August 18 1819 by Prince Leopold of Saxe Coburg'.

➠ *First right enter the gateway to the cemetery.*

Location 2   Old Calton Burial Ground

When laid out, Waterloo Place bisected the cemetery, the south sector of which is larger and contains memorials of greater interest. Outstanding is the cylindrical monument to philosopher David Hume, by Robert Adam, 1777; apparently the Roman tomb of Theodoric at Ravenna was its inspiration. Although designed in 1844, the great obelisk is a memorial to the Political Martyrs of 1793. American soldiers of Scottish descent who took part in the American Civil War are commemorated by the Emancipation Monument of 1893; incorporated is a bronze of a freed slave gazing thankfully at Abraham Lincoln.

➠ *Proceed to the east side of the cemetery.*

Location 3   Former Gaol Governor's House

This castellated house, with its picturesque towers and turrets, is the first Edinburgh building that visitors by rail see as their train emerges from the tunnel on the eastward approach to Waverley Station. Built by Archibald Elliot, 1815–17, it is all that survives of Scotland's largest prison, built to replace the Old Tolbooth's 'Heart of Midlothian'. Elliot's prison formed a long wing, which was supplemented by a castellated penal block designed by Robert Adam.

➠ *Return to Waterloo Place, right. Cross to the north side, pass Calton Hill (the road) junction and ascend the flight of steps left, followed by the next flight, right.*

Location 4   Calton Hill

It is primarily William Playfair's Greek Revival buildings on Calton Hill that have earned Edinburgh the sobriquet 'The Athens of the North'. The hill is 328 ft (100 m) high, and due to its proximity to the city affords unique views across it, which are only slightly marred by the hideous St James Centre at the foot. As early as 1762, Edinburgh had been compared to Athens, both cities being constructed on hills close to the sea; but not until the Napoleonic Wars had ended did its buildings give any real substance to the analogy.

Structures have been placed on Calton Hill's flat summit informally, but at roughly similar intervals; none of them are particularly dominant, and the group does little to detract from the rustic nature of the hill. The entire area provides an unfenced public park; care should be taken after dark as occasional muggings have been reported.

➧ *Proceed to the Nelson Monument at the top of the steps.*

Location 5   Nelson Monument

❖ Open April to September, Monday 1pm to 6pm, Tuesday to Saturday 10am to 6pm; October to March, Monday to Saturday 10am to 3pm. ❖ Admission charge.

The tower was designed by Robert Burn in 1807, originally to provide accommodation for disabled seamen. Surmounting the top stage, a ball is dropped from the mast at noon as a time signal to ships on the Firth of Forth. The strange appearance of the battlemented structure may have been intended to complement James Craig's neo-Gothic Observatory House nearby, which was built 1776–92. It has been likened to an upturned telescope, but there is no evidence that Burn intended this. Visitors may ascend to the top for outstanding views.

➧ *Proceed north-eastward to the unfinished 'Parthenon'.*

Location 6   National Monument

The foundation stone of Scotland's memorial to those who fell in the Napoleonic Wars was laid in 1822, but construction did not begin until 1826; after three years, work was halted, never to resume.

It had been decided that the monument would take the form of a church designed as a replica of the Parthenon on the Athens Acropolis. Charles Cockerell, the architect, was assisted by William Playfair in its completion. Twelve stone columns, including all eight of the west front's, with their base and architrave, had been erected when work ceased. The problem was that less than half the £42,000 required from public subscription had been donated; coincidentally, one of the Scottish promoters of the structure was Lord Elgin, who had been

National Monument and Nelson Monument

much acclaimed for bringing the frieze from the Athens Parthenon (the Elgin marbles) to London's British Museum. Due to the failure of the Scots to complete it, the monument became referred to disparagingly as 'The Shame of Scotland', 'Scotland's Pride and Poverty' and 'Edinburgh's Folly'.

▆▆▶ *Proceed westward to the finished Grecian monument by Playfair at the south-east corner of the City Observatory.*

Professor John Playfair, President of the City Observatory, was the uncle of William Playfair, who designed the monument to him in 1825. Similarities with the Greek Doric Lion Tomb at Cnidos have been noted.

▆▆▶ *Proceed to the south-west corner of the City Observatory.*

Location 7   City Observatory

❖ Open for the 'Edinburgh Experience' (entered from the north-east corner) April to June, September and October, Monday to Friday 2pm to 5pm, Saturdays and Sundays 10.30am to 5pm; July and August daily 10.30am to 5pm.
❖ Admission charge.

Occupying the south-west corner, Observatory House (or the Old Observatory) was the first structure to be built on Calton Hill. Begun in 1776, due to problems with finance it was not completed until 1792. The architect, John Craig, was responsible for laying out Edinburgh's New Town, and this is one of the few buildings designed by him to survive. Allegedly, Robert Adam suggested the fortified appearance of the observatory, which may account for its neo-Gothic windows, corbels and buttresses.

City Observatory itself is the central, domed building, which was commissioned by the Astronomical Institution from William Playfair in 1818. A Greek Cross design was employed, each arm terminating in a Roman Doric portico facing a compass point. The most important function of the observatory was to measure time accurately, but smoke from the trains running below Calton Hill forced the establishment to move to Blackford Hill in 1895.

▆▆▶ *Proceed to the City Dome at the north-east corner.*

This octagonal, domed building, added to the complex in 1895, was designed in neo-classical style by Robert Morham. Visitors are admitted to witness the

Dugald Stewart Monument, with Edinburgh Castle beyond

'Edinburgh Experience', a 20-minute, 3D presentation of the city's history, which requires viewers to wear the usual glasses.

➡ *Exit and return to the south-west corner of the observatory. South of this is Calton Hill's finest monument.*

The Dugald Stewart Monument, designed by Playfair in 1831, closely resembles the Choragic Monument of Lysicrates in Athens. Cylindrical in form, the delicate colonnade and elevated position of this structure has resulted in its inclusion in the foreground of many published views of Edinburgh from the hill. Stewart was a not particularly famous professor of moral philosophy at Edinburgh University, and it is surprising that his monument is so eminent both in content and location.

➡ *Return from Calton Hill to Regent Road by the steps.*

Opposite, the enormous St Andrew's House was designed by Thomas S. Tait and built 1936–39 for the Scottish Office. The architect's love of colossal features, popular at the time, is immediately apparent.

➡ *Continue eastward and cross to the north side of Regent Road.*

Location 8: Royal High School

Regent Road

Some consider this to be the finest of all Edinburgh's Greek Revival buildings – and it is not the work of Playfair. The architect was Thomas Hamilton, who designed a Greek Revival school, which was built 1825-29. It will be noted that the road bends in front of the building and the land slopes in two directions – a nightmare of a site. The porticoed central 'temple' is linked by a colonnade with smaller pavilions at each end.

In 1978, it was expected that a Scottish Parliament would be approved by referendum, and the interior of the school was refitted to accommodate a debating chamber for its use. In the event, the referendum did not ratify the proposal, and the chamber was never used. When approval for devolved government was given by the 1999 referendum, the school was no longer considered suitable for parliamentary use.

➠ *Cross to the south side of Regent Road.*

The Burns Monument, also designed by Hamilton, was erected in 1830 to commemorate Scotland's national poet. Although it is much larger, like Playfair's Dugald Stewart Monument on Calton Hill its design is based on the Choragic Monument of Lysicrates in Athens. A statue of Burns, by John Flaxman, originally stood within the chamber at the monument's base but this is now exhibited in the National Portrait Gallery.

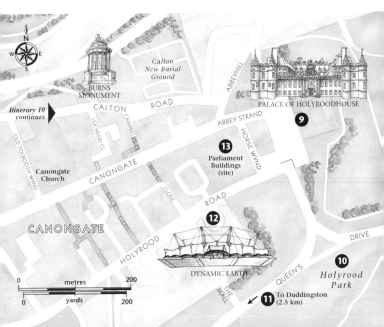

➠ *Descend immediately westward from the Burns Monument, following Calton Hill Stairs. First left, the path falls eastward to Calton Road, left, which ends at Abbeyhill.*

Views over Canongate Churchyard to Holyrood Park are outstanding.

Abbeyhill was laid out in 1857 on the site of the 16th-century Privy Garden of Holyrood Palace. Now cut off from the palace grounds, the two-storey Queen Mary's Bath House, left, dates from the late 16th century. It may have been a summerhouse but certainly never was a bathhouse!

➠ *From the roundabout, Abbey Strand (Itinerary 5) leads to the Palace of Holyroodhouse.*

➠ *Alternatively, particularly if early in the day, proceed directly to Dynamic Earth (Location 12), returning to the palace later.*

Location 9:   The Palace of Holyroodhouse

❖ Open daily April to October 9.30am to 5.15pm, November to March 9.30am to 3.45pm. ❖ Admission charge. ❖ Holyrood is not open to the public when members of the royal family are in residence; the Queen usually spends at least one week at Holyrood in July.

After Edinburgh Castle, Holyroodhouse is the city's most historic building. Visitors are shown the 17th-century state apartments built for Charles II (who never saw Holyrood) and Mary, Queen of Scots' chambers, which are located in the 16th-century tower built by her father James V. As the tour ends with the ruined nave of the late 12th-century abbey church, this is described as if it were a separate entity.

The Royal Palace

A royal guesthouse was probably established at Holyrood soon after the abbey's foundation in 1128, but reference to its existence was first made in 1329. The birth, coronation, marriage and burial of James II at Holyrood indicate that a royal palace of importance had evolved beside the abbey by the 15th century. In 1515, prior to his marriage with Margaret Tudor, James IV rebuilt the palace in the form of a quadrangle to the south of the abbey church and west of the monastic cloister, a layout that remains little changed to this day. In 1532 his son, James V, added a tower in the north-west corner to house the royal apartments, and rebuilt the remainder of the palace four years later.

The Earl of Hertford's English troops sacked Edinburgh in 1544 (Henry VIII's 'Rough Wooing' to secure a match between his son, Edward, and Mary, Queen of Scots) and Holyrood was badly damaged. Repairs had been made when Mary returned to Scotland from France in 1561, and the queen occupied the second floor of the tower built by her father until shortly before here forced abdication in 1567. Her son and successor James VI also held court at Holyroodhouse, but on inheriting the throne of England in 1603 departed for London, only returning for a brief 'Hamecoming' fourteen years later. Although Charles I was crowned King of Scotland at Holyrood in 1633, ever a traditionalist he spent the night before the ceremony at Edinburgh Castle. While Cromwell's troops occupied the palace as barracks in 1650, the east wing was badly damaged by a fire.

Following the Restoration of the Monarchy in 1660, Charles II ordered the west range and the tower to be repaired for occupation by the King's Commissioner to the newly-revived Scottish Parliament, and William Bruce's plan for completely rebuilding the remainder, apart from the west wing, in classical style was approved in 1671. Five years later, the west range was similarly rebuilt, but James V's north-west tower was retained and little altered. The king's brother, James, Duke of York, occupied the new Great Apartment in the west range in 1691, even though it was not quite finished. Other brief occupants included Bonnie Prince Charlie in 1745 and the Comte d'Artois, brother of the guillotined Louis XVI of France, in 1796. George IV gave receptions at Holyrood during his state visit to Scotland in 1822 but slept elsewhere.

The Palace of Holyroodhouse

It was not until Queen Victoria stayed at Holyrood in 1850, en route to her newly-acquired Balmoral Castle, that royal interest in the palace truly revived. In 1871 a permanent apartment was created for the queen on the second floor, and this is still occupied by the sovereign when in residence.

Exterior

The forecourt is entered from the Abbey Courthouse, which was rebuilt by Robert Reid in 1823. On its north wall, blind arcading and the arms of James V from the gatehouse built by James IV in 1502 have been incorporated; the remainder of that picturesque building was senselessly demolished in 1753.

Lying back on the north side is the abbey church, which can be approached more closely at the end of the tour.

The north-west tower survives from James V's Scottish Renaissance palace, built 1528–32. When it was restored in 1676, the casement windows were replaced by sashes and their protective iron grilles removed. Originally, the tower could only be entered via an iron drawbridge, a defensive measure reinforced by the gun-loops on the ground floor. Stone panels on the first floor of the turrets are carved, respectively, with the arms of James V and Mary of Guise, both 1906 reproductions of the originals, and of James V, a copy of the panel seen on the wall of the courthouse.

Bruce's west range, built 1676–79, links the north-west and south-west towers. To the rear it may be observed that the rest of the palace is one storey plus an attic floor higher. The only feature of much interest in the west range is its centre-piece: a Doric entrance, with Charles II's monogram, thistles and the Scottish regalia carved on its frieze. Immediately above the doorway, the massive sculpted coat of arms was designed by Jacob de Wet in 1677. Above this a crowned cupola encloses a clock dated 1680.

Before entering the palace, it may be noted that the south-west tower was designed by Bruce as a twin (apart from being given a doorway) to the older tower; as may be expected, the better condition of its ashlar stonework immediately proclaims this tower's more recent construction.

➠ *Enter the palace and turn right.*

Seen immediately is the internal, grassed quadrangle, its central stone lamp standard of 1908 based on 17th-century Scottish designs. The ground floor is arcaded, and classical orders in the approved ascending form of Doric, Ionic and Corinthian pilasters separate each bay. On the east range, a pediment is carved with the monogram and coat of arms of Charles II.

An 18th-century sedan chair usually stands in the vestibule at the foot of the stairs. However, it should be borne in mind that changes to the interiors of the palace are made from time to time.

➠ *Ascend the Great Stair to the first floor.*

The Great Stair

The four 16th-century Brussels tapestries from The Planets series were brought to Holyrood from Hampton Court around 1860. Framed sections of North Italian frescoes transferred to canvas are the work of Lattanzio Gambara, c1530–74, which came to the palace from London in 1888. Most of the sumptuous plasterwork of the ceilings in the royal apartments at Holyrood is the work of two Englishmen, John Houlbert and George Dunsterfield. All were meant to incorporate a central painting, but due to financial restrictions only one was executed. From Houlbert's work above the staircase it is immediately apparent that in contrast with its severely classical exterior, Holyrood internally is exuberantly Baroque.

➠ *Proceed ahead.*

Royal Dining Room

Planned as the Queen's Guardroom, this area originally marked the beginning of her suite of rooms. During his exile at Holyrood, the Comte d'Artois commissioned new furniture from Edinburgh craftsmen; surviving from his acquisitions in this room are the pair of mahogany pier tables against the west wall. The dining chairs are late 18th-century and the dining table early 19th-century. On the north wall hangs the famous portrait of George IV in Highland Dress, by Sir David Wilkie. The king's pink tights beneath his kilt were an idiosyncratic choice of garment. Above the fireplace hangs a painting of the 19-year-old Queen Victoria, by Sir George Hayter, 1838.

➠ *Return towards the Great Stair and turn left to enter the Great (King's) Apartment.*

Throne Room

Charles II's Guardroom was adapted for the visit of George IV in 1822 to become the Great Drawing Room. Seated on a throne that had been made for his mother, Queen Charlotte, the king was presented with the rediscovered crown of Scotland. The chimneypiece dates from 1856, but the plaster ceiling and 17th-century-style wood panelling were installed in 1929. The present thrones, bearing the monograms GR and MR, were made for George V and Queen Mary in 1911. Royal portraits in the room depict Stuart monarchs and two of their consorts.

Evening Drawing Room

Originally the King's Presence Chamber, the 17th-century-style wood panelling in this room dates from the 1930s, whereas the panelling in the four rooms that follow is original.

The four mid-18th-century French armchairs and sofa are upholstered in Beauvais tapestry-work depicting the fairy tales of Fontaine. Above the fireplace, the portrait of Queen Elizabeth The Queen Mother was painted by Sir William Hutchinson in 1967. The mid-18th-century Brussels tapestries from the Four Continents series were transferred here from Buckingham Palace.

Morning Drawing Room

Formerly the King's Privy Chamber, the decor here is the most extravagant yet seen; it reflects the original order of progression through the Great Apartment, in which the rooms gradually increased in importance. Dutch sculptor Jan van Santvoort was responsible for the sumptuous carving of the chimneypiece; its Cupid and Psyche painting is by de Wet. In each corner of the magnificent ceiling, the cypher of Charles II appears within a wreath. The four tapestries, made in Paris around 1630, are from a series illustrating the History of Diana.

King's Ante-Chamber

In this room the panelling and plasterwork are less exuberant, reflecting its smaller scale. Above the fireplace, the de Wet painting portrays *The Triumph of Galatea*. The two late 16th-century Flemish tapestries from the Aeneid series are known to have been at Holyrood as early as 1685; as in the previous room, Paris tapestries are from the History of Diana series. Re-upholstered late 17th-century chairs are set around the room; the 16th-century marquetry cabinet is German.

King's Bedchamber

Undoubtedly the finest room at Holyroodhouse, the King's Bedchamber is a Baroque masterpiece; only here did the ceiling receive its intended painting: de Wet's *Apotheosis of Hercules*. On the chimneypiece, de Wet portrays *The Infant Hercules Strangling the Serpents*.

Displayed in the chamber is the four-poster bed, dating from around 1680, which belonged to the Duke of Hamilton; most of its drapes have been renewed. Also from the late 17th century are the four armchairs, walnut pier tables, walnut mirrors and candle stands. Both tapestries, from the History of Alexander series, were made in Brussels early in the 17th century.

The Lobby

This small lobby originally gave access to the King's Stool Room, in which his toilet was located.

King's Closet

Designed for use by the king as his private study, this, the last chamber in the Great Apartment, was the only one that could be regarded as truly private in the modern sense. The ceiling is coved, its corners decorated with trophies of war, and the cove itself with Charles II's monogram.

An ancient Scottish myth is that their kings were descended from Scota, the Pharaoh's daughter who discovered the infant Moses in the bullrushes: accordingly, this provides the theme of de Wet's overmantel painting.

An 18th-century harpsichord and an early 19th-century harp, both French, now give the King's Closet the appearance of a music room. From the late 17th century are: the five chairs, two gilded candle stands, a pier table, a pier glass and the Mortlake tapestries depicting four scenes from the Life of Diogenes.

Great Gallery

Charles II insisted that a passageway should link the Great Apartment with the Queen's Apartment in the north-west tower. The 'passageway' became the Grand Gallery; its internal north wall (right) appears to be the reused north wall of James V's palace.

There is some 17th-century Classical detailing in the Great Gallery, which is the largest room in the palace, but the ceiling had been plain until decoration was added in 1968 to mitigate its 'tunnel-like' appearance.

Jacob de Wet was commissioned in 1684 to paint the portraits of Scotland's 110 monarchs, some of them legendary, from Fergus I to Charles II; James VII was a subsequent addition. The work took the Dutchman just two years to complete – at the rate of one painting per week – but the 'portraits' of the early kings are entirely conjectural. It is said that de Wet was instructed to maintain a 'Stuart look' throughout to support the dynasty's claim of a divine right to rule. As specified, each painting bears the name, age and length of reign of the monarch in question; Mary, Queen of Scots is erroneously shown to have been born a year later than she actually was (1543 rather than 1542).

Bonnie Prince Charlie held receptions in the Great Gallery during his short-lived occupancy of Holyrood in 1745, but later in the same year English troops took over the palace and slashed the portraits of the monarchs with their sabres.

Subsequently restored, the paintings were removed from their frames in 1826, eventually being fitted into the wall panels created for them.

The chairs are late 17th-century.

Queen's Lobby

Apart from Queen Mary's Chambers in the north-west tower this is the only royal chamber to survive from James V's 16th-century palace, in which it served as the King's Wardrobe. However, William Bruce completely refitted the room in 1671 as the Queen's Privy Chamber, including a new ceiling by James Baine.

Tam O'Shanter's brass-panelled chair was made early in the 19th century.

Queen's Ante-Chamber

Located on the first floor of James V's tower, and originally the King's Outer Chamber, the room was also remodelled by Bruce in 1672. During the early part of his marriage to Mary, Queen of Scots, Lord Darnley occupied this and the adjacent chamber.

The four 17th-century Mortlake tapestries are from the Playing Boys series. Above the fireplace, the portrait of the 2nd Duke of Hamilton was painted around 1650. Two portraits of the Old Pretender are usually displayed.

Queen's Bedchamber

Also located within James V's tower, this room was originally the King's Bedchamber.

While occupying Holyrood, Bonnie Prince Charlie slept in this room; his bed, the half-tester that remains on display, is believed to have been purchased by the Duke of Hamilton in 1682. Much of its upholstery is original, which is why protective glass has been fitted and the room's blinds are kept drawn.

Above the fireplace hangs a posthumous portrait of the young James, Duke of Cambridge, painted around 1685.

Ascend the spiral staircase to Mary, Queen of Scots' Chambers, beginning with her bedchamber.

Mary, Queen of Scots' Bedchamber

Behind a glass panel, in the corner left of the entrance, is the privy stair, which linked Darnley's rooms with Queen Mary's. It has been said, however, that the original staircase was straight rather than spiral. In 1566, Darnley led the conspirators via the stair to the Queen's Supper Room in search of Rizzio. After returning to Scotland from France in 1561, Queen Mary occupied the four rooms on the tower's second floor as her private apartment. The Duke of Hamilton subsequently incorporated them in his much larger suite, and a century later visits by members of the public were permitted. The timber ceiling is early 16th-century work, but the royal cyphers MR and IR (Mary, Queen of Scots and James VI) carved on the bosses were probably added in 1617 for James VI's 'Hamecoming'. The CR and CP initials of Charles I and Charles, Prince of Wales were almost certainly painted in 1633 for the Scottish coronation at Holyrood of Charles I. A Jacobean grey-painted frieze on the wall depicts the Honours of Scotland; again, this probably dates from 1617; most of it was not discovered until 1976.

Most of the paintings in this room date from the 16th and 17th centuries; predominantly they are royal portraits or depict religious themes. Beside the south window is a view of the room painted in 1861. An inscription on a Flemish cabinet erroneously proclaims that it belonged to Mary, Queen of Scots; it is, in fact, 17th-century work. From the late 17th century are the bed hangings, two 'stools' beside the bed with their original covers and four Antwerp tapestries from The History of Phaeton series.

Supper Room

The 12 ft (4 m) square north turret room (entry barred by a rope) is the Supper Room in which Queen Mary, Rizzio and the Countess of Argyll were among those about to dine when seven assassins burst in led by Lord Darnley, followed by Lord Ruthven, who wore armour. Original hangings in the room have survived due to their being kept under glass since the 19th century. From the mid-16th century are two paintings by Veronese: *David defeating Goliath* and *Judith with the Head of Holofernes*. Flemish late 17th-century tapestries depict forest scenes. A second turret room of identical proportions in the south-west corner, originally a dressing room, is closed as it now serves as a first-aid centre – more than four centuries too late to be of help to poor Rizzio!

Mary, Queen of Scots' Outer Chamber

The ceiling to this adjacent, slightly larger room was probably made 1528–32. Its coats of arms, although made in 1559, were brought from elsewhere in 1617. They include those of Mary, Queen of Scots, her mother Mary of Guise, James V, James VI, Henri II (HR) of France and his son Francois II (FD). The D denotes that the youth was still Dauphin when, at the age of fourteen, he married Queen Mary.

➠ *Proceed clockwise.*

In the centre of the west (entrance) wall, the portrait of Queen Mary is a posthumous 18th-century work, but displayed in the cabinet below it is the famous miniature portrait of her, painted from life by François Clouet in 1559. In the same cabinet are examples of Mary's needlework and a lock of her hair.

A painting of Lord Darnley, together with his brother Charles, hangs to the left of the first north window. Depicted to the right of the second north window, Don Carlos, son of Philip II of Spain, was for a short time considered as a possible match for Queen Mary. Below this, the 17th-century painting is said to be a posthumous portrait of David Rizzio; however, by all accounts he was a remarkably unattractive looking man, and no longer youthful when employed by the queen. A plaque below records that 'his body was left here'.

Lord Darnley had been persuaded that Rizzio was not only his wife's secretary and musician but also her lover, and although a Catholic, he took part in the conspiracy by leading Protestants to assassinate Rizzio in Mary's suite of rooms. Rizzio appears to have been dragged from the Supper Room through the Bedchamber to the queen's Outer Chamber and stabbed 56 times before expiring in front of the 'Historic Staircase' at the end of the room on 9 March 1566.

Among the paintings on the south wall, the group portrait of King Henry VII's family with St George and the Dragon is a Flemish work painted around 1507, two years before the king's death.

Between the north and south walls are displayed: the exquisite Darnley Jewel, made for Lord Darnley's mother around 1570, and the jewelled accoutrements of George IV.

➠ *Descend by the 16th-century Historic Staircase to the Quadrant, left, and proceed to the ruined nave of the abbey church, which is entered from its south-west corner.*

Between October and April, paintings from the Royal Collection on varying themes are displayed in the first floor's outer rooms on the south side of the palace and may be seen before reaching the church.

Holyrood Abbey

By tradition, while hunting on 14 September 1128 King David I was charged by a huge stag and fell from his horse. Raising his hand towards the stag's menacing antlers, the king found himself clutching a fragment of the True Cross: the stag had disappeared. In gratitude, the king founded Holyrood Abbey where the event had occurred. The new monastery was served by Augustinian canons from Merton Abbey, near London, the small church of which provided the model for what would be built at Holyrood.

Around 1190 a far more imposing church was commissioned, its scale and magnificence rivalling that of many a cathedral; for almost 450 years this would provide the venue for a variety of major royal events. At the Reformation the abbey was suppressed and its monastic buildings abandoned. The transepts and chancel of the church were demolished, but the nave was spared because it served as the parish church of Canongate burgh. The last major event within the building was the Scottish coronation of Charles I, in 1633, for which it was patched up. James VII, a devout Catholic, planned to convert the church to the chapel of the revived Order of the Thistle, but he was deposed in 1688, before the work could be finished. In 1768 the ten-year-old stone slab roof of the building collapsed, bringing down much of the structure.

Before losing its chancel and transepts at the Reformation, the abbey church was almost twice the length of its nave, which is the only part to have survived, albeit in a ruinous condition. Now filled with window tracery and additional stonework, the apertures in the east wall were formerly archways that gave access to the crossing, transepts and chancel.

Apart from its north-west bay, the wall of the north aisle is decorated with a delightful blind arcade of interlacing rounded arches, a Romanesque feature in what is otherwise a Gothic church, indicating that it was built at a transitional stage.

At the east end, the present window tracery dates from the restoration of the church for the coronation of Charles I in 1633 (renewed in 1816). Below the north aisle's window, the late 15th-century stone screen bears the arms of Abbot Crawford, 1460–83, who was responsible for rebuilding the vault of the roof.

The east bay of the south aisle now accommodates the royal vault, which contains the unidentified remains of some of those who had been buried in the church, including several Scottish kings. Beside this stands the imposing Hamilton family vault.

➡ *Exit from the church to view the east end of Holyrood (from March to September only).*

Flying buttresses on the south side of the nave were part of Abbot Crawford's 15th-century alterations designed to improve the stability of the building. Originally, flyers supported the wall of the nave in addition to its aisle. Also in this wall can be seen a blocked Romanesque processional doorway, all that survives from the original 12th-century church; its scalloped capitals and dog-tooth decoration are typical of the period. To the east of the church are the excavated foundations of its transepts and chancel; also discernible is the outline of the east end of the earlier church.

⟱▶ *Return through the church and exit to view its west front.*

What survives of the west front represents only one-third of the original. The two main reasons for this were the construction of the palace for Charles II, which necessitated the demolition of the south parts, and the collapse of 1768 in which the upper stages, remodelled for Charles I, were lost. However, with the exception of the cusping of the two large windows, and the carved wooden lintel above the entrance, part of the 1633 additions, the structure retains its original 13th-century appearance. Influenced by the contemporary Early English style, the facade is profusely decorated with blind arcading featuring lancet arches. The deep, richly-carved portal is reminiscent of northern French cathedrals.

⟱▶ *From Holyroodhouse exit ahead to Abbey Strand. First left Horse Wynd. First left Holyrood Road. Right Queen's Drive (which circumnavigates Holyrood Park).*

Location 10   Holyrood Park (or Queen's Park)

The park is roughly circular, with a diameter of approximately 5 miles (8 km). It is a royal foundation, which was extended to its present size by James V, 1541–42. Queen's Drive has two further intersections: south-west at Holyrood Park Road (for Duddingston) and north-east at Duke's Walk, for London Road. Although only a short distance from the city centre, Holyrood Park, which is unfenced, provides a microcosm of Scottish scenery, with mountains, crags, moorland, marshes and rocks, and in consequence it is extremely popular with Edinburgh hikers seeking exercise that is neither too far distant nor too strenuous. The three easiest paths for walkers are: the 'Radical Road', from opposite the south gate of the palace, which follows Salisbury Crags southward; Hunter's Bog, from St Margaret's Well to the southern tip of Salisbury Crags; and Long Row, from the ruined St Anthony's Chapel to Arthur's Seat and Dunsapie Loch. Private vehicles are permitted to use Queen's Drive, but not commercial vehicles (including buses).

Seen immediately left of the road, Salisbury Crags is a lengthy rampart, which gave protection to the prehistoric fort once situated behind it. Arthur's Seat, further east, rises 823 ft (251 m) above sea level and is Edinburgh's best-known natural landmark. Like Castle Rock, it is also an extinct volcano, and is most easily approached on foot – a 20-minute walk – from Dunsapie Loch to the east.

⟱▶ *To approach Samson's Crags and Duddingston Village by car it is necessary to return westward a short distance and turn left at the roundabout. First left, Old Church Lane.*

Samson's Ribs, left of the road, comprises stone pillars of volcanic origin: traces of a small fort lie to the rear.

Location 11   Duddingston

The road soon passes, right, the north side of Duddingston Loch, which has been designated a bird sanctuary.

Overlooking the water, Duddingston Kirk, although mostly 17th century, is a 12th-century foundation, and two Romanesque features of importance have survived. Although now much-faded, the Norman doorway, at the west end of the nave's south wall, incorporates some exceptional carving, including a crucifixion scene. Within, the chancel arch has the usual dog-tooth pattern and scallop capitals.

Near the church is the Manse of 1805 and a house built by Playfair in 1823 for the Rev John Thorne, who apparently named it Edinburgh so that if unwelcome callers arrived, servants could truthfully tell them he was 'in Edinburgh'. More famous, however, is the plain, greatly restored No. 8 The Causeway, built in 1721, in which Bonnie Prince Charlie is said to have spent the night before his victory at the Battle of Prestonpans in 1745. Also in The Causeway is the Sheep Heid, a picturesque inn, built in 1670, and said to be the country's oldest licensed premises.

Buses 42 and 46 from Duddingston Road West return to Edinburgh centre.

Those with a vehicle who wish to complete the circuit of Holyrood Park must return to Queen's Drive and turn right. To the right, on the east side of the park, Dunsapie Loch is backed by Dunsapie Hill, to the east of which are the remains of a fort. Queen's Drive bears north passing, left, St Margaret's Loch, created in the 19th century. On a crag above it are the ruins of the medieval St Anthony's Chapel.

Just before the right turn-off to Holyrood Palace, and set in an enclosure on the slope beside the road, St Margaret's Well is a hexagonal room, probably dating from the late 15th century, which was brought to the park from Restalrig in 1859.

➠ *First right Queen's Drive returns northward towards the palace. First left Holyrood Road.*

Location 12   Dynamic Earth

Holyrood Road

❖ Open daily Easter to October 10am to 6pm; November to Easter, Wednesday to Sunday 10am to 5pm. ❖ Admission charge. ❖ Visitors must usually expect to wait for the nearest 'time-slot' before their tour can begin.

Funded by donations and lottery money, Dynamic Earth is Edinburgh's major

Dynamic Earth and Salisbury Crags

contribution to the millennium celebrations. It is neither a museum nor an exhibition, but a permanent visitor attraction that dramatically shows how Earth has been created and shaped through time by the interaction of disparate forces.

Backed by the appropriately 'geological' Salisbury Crags, Dynamic Earth is accommodated within a three-level structure roofed by a translucent, gleaming-white tent, which is cleaned naturally by rain. Opened in 1999, the building was designed by Sir Michael Hopkins.

Descend to the mezzanine level, in which the **Present state of the Earth** is explained: weather conditions (including earthquakes) and births and deaths throughout the world are monitored. Up to 35 visitors can board the **'Time Machine'** video lift, which descends slowly to the ground floor. Images of historic events scroll back faster and faster from the present through 15 billion years to the Big Bang. From the bridge of a 'starship', visitors are shown **How it all Started**, meteor storms and exploding gases ending with the formation of the planet. **Restless Earth** explains on three enormous floor-to-ceiling screens how movement and destruction have moulded the planet. When earthquakes and volcanos are depicted, the floor shakes and a sulphurous odour fills the chamber. On five large screens, **Shaping the Surface** includes film of a helicopter's low flight across Norwegian glaciers, and is for many the highlight of their visit. **Casualties and Survivors** explains how life evolved, while a submarine 'voyage' is the highlight of **Oceans**. In **Polar Regions**, cold temperatures are encountered by visitors, who can touch an iceberg, observe a polar bear diving and be deafened by a colony of squawking penguins. **Tundra to Tropical** examines areas that are again depicted on huge screens; a popular feature of the **Tropical Rainforest** is its quarter-hourly rainstorm – with real, very wet, water.

➽ *Exit directly ahead from the building.*

An open-air natural stone amphitheatre seating a thousand faces Dynamic Earth. In summer, particularly during the Festival, programmes of special events are arranged.

➽ *Cross to the north side of Holyrood Road.*

Location 13   Parliament Buildings

Holyrood Road/Canongate

Scheduled to open in the autumn of 2001, the new complex for the Scottish Parliament will occupy around four acres bounded by Holyrood Road, Horse Wynd, Canongate and Reids Close. Like Dynamic Earth, most of the site was formerly the premises of a brewery, but it also incorporates the 17th-century Queensberry House, which is to be restored (see page 72) and will provide the members' entrance.

In July 1998, Catalan architect Enric Miralles, in partnership with his wife and the Edinburgh-based RMJM, was judged winner of the international competition to design the new Parliament Buildings. The final model of the complex can be seen at the Visitor Centre on George IV Bridge (see page 78). Demolition of existing structures was completed in July 1999 and building commenced.

In view of their beautiful and historic location, Parliament Buildings have been designed as a group of individual units that are sensitive to the scale of Queensbery House. Of greatest interest to the public will be the Debating Chamber, which is to be located at the eastern extremity of the site, immediately facing Holyrood Palace. Access to the visitors' and press galleries will be provided nearby.

➽ *To return to the city centre it is better to follow Reid's Close (marking the west end of the Parliament Buildings site) northward to Canongate. If walking turn left, if taking the bus turn right for the stop.*

Dean, Stockbridge and the Northern New Town

The Scottish National Gallery of Modern Art – The Dean Gallery –
Water of Leith – Royal Botanic Garden – Royal Circus – Moray Estate

This itinerary, which concentrates on the north-west sector of central
Edinburgh, comprises two former riverside villages and the Northern New
Town which borders them. Most of the route follows the footpath along
the narrow gorge-like river known as the Water of Leith. No great individ-
ual buildings are passed, but the Georgian squares and terraces of the
Northern New Town are the least spoiled in the city.

Timing: *Both art galleries open daily at 10am except Sundays (2pm), and the state of
the weather for visiting them is, of course, irrelevant. However, the remainder of the itinerary,
especially the Royal Botanic Garden, which opens daily at 10am, demands a fine day.*

Start: *The Scottish National Gallery of Modern Art, Belford Road. Bus 13 from the
south-west corner of Charlotte Square (roughly a 30 minute service) passes the gallery. In*

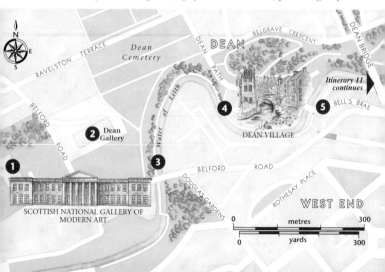

1999 an experimental complimentary bus service linked Edinburgh's five national galleries; check the current situation as this depended on continued sponsorship.

Location 1   The Scottish National Gallery of Modern Art

Belford Road

❖ Open Monday to Saturday 10am to 5pm, Sunday 2pm to 5pm. ❖ Admission free, apart from special major exhibitions.

In spite of the apparent immensity of its premises, the gallery can only exhibit a small percentage of its collection of 4,000 items at one time. A system of rotation has therefore been employed, and it cannot be assumed that any particular work will be on view during a specific period. The situation eased somewhat in March 1999 when the gallery's outstanding collection of Surrealist and Dada works, together with Paolozzi sculptures, was transferred to the Dean Gallery opposite.

Many visitors approaching the gallery through its spacious grounds, in which sculptures are displayed, believe that they are confronted by a former stately home: in fact it was built as a school. William Burn designed John Watson's School in the 1820s as a two-storey-above-basement building in Greek Revival classical style, featuring a central pedimented portico; the boys' dormitories occupied the first floor. The building was adapted in 1984 to house the Modern Art Collection.

French paintings and German Expressionism are the gallery's greatest attractions, with superb works by Matisse, Vuillard, Picasso, Léger and Feininger. Contemporary works by British artists such as Bacon, Hockney and Alan Davie, and 20th century Scots – Charles Rennie Mackintosh, Fergusson and Gillies – are naturally featured. French Impressionists and Postimpressionists are generally exhibited in the Scottish National Gallery on the Mound.

➠ *Exit and cross to the east side of Belford Road.*

Location 2   The Dean Gallery

Belford Road

❖ Open Monday to Saturday 10am to 5pm, Sunday 2pm to 5pm. ❖ Admission free.

The Dean Gallery opened in 1999, primarily to house the Paolozzi Gift of Edinburgh-born sculptor Eduardo Paolozzi. It is accommodated in the grandest of all the Edinburgh galleries, originally built as an orphanage for boys and girls.

Thomas Hamilton designed the building 1831–33 with his favoured 'temple' centrepiece. Comprising two storeys above a terrace, detailing is severely neo-classical until the English Baroque superstructures are reached. Set on the two-stage attic behind the pediment is a clock said to have been saved from Edinburgh's demolished Netherbow Port; its boldly carved supports and crest are typical of the late-George IV/William IV period. However, it is the two open towers that startle; their lowest stages provide light to the two internal staircases, while the octagonal shafts above served as ornamental chimneys: all very Vanbrughian. The gallery's permanent collection is displayed on the ground floor, while its top floor is reserved for temporary exhibitions. Rooms of greatest interest to most flank the main entrance; the Eduardo Paolozzi exhibits include a re-creation of his London studio. Bequests from Sir Roland Penrose and Gabrielle Keiller have provided the Dean Gallery with one of the world's finest collections of Surrealist and Dada art. Represented are: Dalí, Ernst, Magritte, Miró, Man Ray, Tanguy, Delvaux and Picasso.

➠ *Exit left and follow Belford Road southward to the Hilton Hotel. Cross to the north side of the road and descend beside Belford Bridge to the footpath, which follows the Water of Leith.*

Location 3   Water of Leith

The Water of Leith is a narrow river which rises in the Pentland Hills, south-west of Edinburgh, from where it flows eastward to Leith and the Firth of Forth. Along its banks, villages such as Colinton, Dean and Stockbridge used the river for centuries to power grain mills, distilleries and tanneries, but in the late 19th century these industries became confined mostly to Leith, where much larger units had been constructed. As may be expected, the decline of their industry led to much dilapidation in and around the villages, and not until World War II had ended did many of them begin to recover. Within walking distance of Edinburgh centre, and yet rural in appearance – as opposed to the formal urbanity of the adjacent Northern New Town – the attraction of Water of Leith properties became apparent, and they now provide most fashionable addresses, particularly if located in Dean or Stockbridge.

A footpath, the Water of Leith Walkway, has been created alongside the river, and those so inclined may follow it all the way to Leith; however, the section between Dean and Stockbridge is the most scenic, as well as the most accessible from Edinburgh.

➠ *Follow the riverside path, crossing to the opposite side as indicated.*

Location 4　Dean

Dean evolved in the 12th century, following the construction of grain mills along the riverside. At the height of its industrial period 11 mills were in operation providing flour for the region; no mills remain but some remnants of them, converted to other uses, have survived. Surprisingly, an 18th-century tannery existed at Dean until the early 1920s. Although Dean has few buildings of outstanding architectural interest, its setting, in which the river bends through a cleft, is outstandingly picturesque.

➠ *Cross the iron footbridge to the south side. Left, Hawthornbank Lane leads to Bell's Brae.*

Location 5　Bell's Brae

Until Dean Bridge was constructed in 1832, Bell's Brae, with its 18th-century bridge, served as the main road from Edinburgh to Queensferry and the north.

The four storey Nos 11–13, The Baxters' Tolbooth, was built in 1675 as a granary and their headquarters by the Incorporation of Baxters (Bakers). Over the west door are carved a wheatsheaf, cherubs' heads, a pie, weighing scales and inscriptions. Stair turrets were restored with crowsteps when the building was converted to flats in 1976.

➠ *Proceed to the upper end of Bell's Brae (Randolph Cliff).*

Kirkbrae House was built in the late 17th century as 'The Baxters House of Call', a tavern for the local bakers; in 1892 it was linked with a newly-built Scottish baronial mansion, and the pair make a picturesque ensemble. Brought from other Dean properties are the sculpted head of a judge and an appropriate inscription from Genesis; both are early 17th-century carvings. Those 17th-century bakers were lucky to have a 'House of Call' as pubs are no longer permitted in Dean.

Miller Row's name commemorates the flour mills that survived along it until the 1950s.

➠ *Follow Bell's Brae eastward. First left Dean Bridge.*

Dean Bridge, 148 yd (136 m) long, was built by Thomas Telford in 1832 to form an important part of the Queensferry Road link between the Firth of Forth and Edinburgh. In 1912 the bridge parapets were heightened to dissuade people from jumping off them. On the north side of the bridge the neo-Gothic Holy Trinity Church was built in 1838; it has been little altered externally, even though conversion to an electricity transformer station took place in 1957 – and now, remarkably, has been re-converted to its original ecclesiastical use.

Dean Village lies west of Holy Trinity, but there are no period buildings as one might expect; most are Victorian or modern replacements. The original Dean Village, first called Water of Leith Village, lay slightly further north but has been built over.

➠ *Return to the riverside path and continue north-eastward.*

Beside the river, St George's Well, dated 1810, was named to celebrate the jubilee of George III.

More impressive is St Bernard's Well, slightly further north, which was designed as a circular Roman Doric pumphouse by Alexander Nasmyth in 1788. This replaced a small well of 1760 and was commissioned by Lord Gardenstone, who claimed to have derived benefit from its mineral water. The present statue of Hygeia replaced the original in 1888. Below the 'temple' structure the pump-house itself is occasionally open to visitors, tel: 0131 445-7367.

➠ *Continue ahead to St Bernard's Bridge and cross the Water of Leith to Stockbridge. First right Dean Terrace.*

Location 6   Stockbridge

Originally, like Dean, a riverside mill village, Stockbridge began to expand in 1813 when its first Georgian streets were built. However, the scale was much smaller and the layout much less formal than the New Town's. In consequence, Stockbridge gives the impression of a country town rather than an Edinburgh suburb. In recent years its shops, restaurants and pubs have become fashionable venues.

Location 7   Raeburn Estate

The sudden 19th-century development of Stockbridge was almost entirely due to the entrepreneurial abilities of the famous painter Sir Henry Raeburn (1756–1823). Although born in Stockbridge to an artisan family, he acquired wealth by his marriage in 1780 to Anne Edgar, a rich widow who had inherited the Deanhaugh Estate. However, not until 1813 were plots of building land made available to purchasers. Much of the scheme was designed by James Mylne, but how much is unclear. Although there is no evidence, it is hard to believe that Raeburn himself did not influence architectural detail. When completed, the Raeburn Estate included a triangular development wedged between the south bank of the Water of Leith and the Northern New Town development, but this was almost entirely demolished in the iconoclastic 1960s.

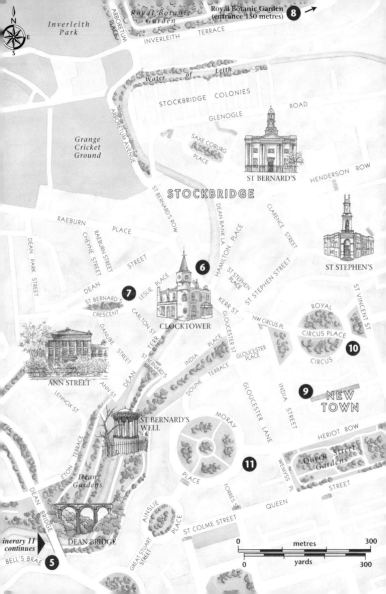

Inverleith
Park

Royal Botanic
Garden

Royal Botanic Garden
(entrance 150 metres) **8**

INVERLEITH   TERRACE

Water   of   Leith

STOCKBRIDGE COLONIES

GLENOGLE   ROAD

SAXE COBURG
PLACE

ST BERNARD'S

HENDERSON   ROW

STOCKBRIDGE

Grange
Cricket
Ground

ARBORETUM AVENUE

ST BERNARD'S ROW

DEAN BANK LA.

HAMILTON PLACE

CLARENCE   STREET

ST STEPHEN'S

RAEBURN   PLACE

CHEYNE STREET

RAEBURN STREET

STREET

DEAN PARK STREET

DEAN   STREET

ST BERNARD'S

CRESCENT

7

LESLIE PLACE

CARLTON ST

ST STEPHEN
PLACE

ST STEPHEN STREET

KERR ST

NW CIRCUS PL

ST VINCENT ST

ROYAL

CIRCUS PLACE

6

CLOCKTOWER

GLOUCESTER ST

GLOUCESTER PLACE

CIRCUS

10

ANN STREET

DANUBE   STREET

ANN ST

DEAN

ST BERNARD'S BRIDGE

TERR

INDIA   PLACE

DOUNE   TERRACE

GLOUCESTER   LANE

INDIA   STREET

9   **NEW
TOWN**

LENNOX ST

ST BERNARD'S
WELL

HERIOT   ROW

MORAY   PLACE

WEMYSS PL

Queen Street
Gardens

ETON   TERRACE

Dean Gardens

PLACE

11

STREET

FORRES ST

QUEEN

Itinerary II
continues
5

BELL'S BRAE

DEAN   BRIDGE

DEAN BRIDGE

AINSLIE

GREAT STUART STREET

PLACE

ST COLME STREET

0   metres   300

0   yards   300

The following route takes in the streets of greatest interest, but some visitors may wish to explore more comprehensively if time permits.

Carlton Street, *first left,* was laid out in 1826 after the demolition of St Bernard's House, which had stood close to its east side and had been Raeburn's home.

St Bernard's Crescent, *left,* was apparently suggested by Raeburn's fellow painter Sir David Wilkie, and its Greek Doric three-storey centrepiece is astonishingly grand for a residential development. The two-storey, balustraded houses have been given a continuous colonnade, but it is obvious that the scheme was never quite completed as designed. Work began in 1824, shortly after Raeburn's death.

Danube Street, *first left,* has been judged the most attractive Greek Revival street in Edinburgh, primarily due to the contrasting rural and urban views provided. From its north end the street gently swings eastward.

➠ *First right Upper Dean Terrace. First right Ann Street.*

Many consider Ann Street to be the most attractive place to live in Edinburgh due to its hillside location and long front gardens, a feature that previously had existed nowhere else in the city. The street's name is undoubtedly a gesture made by Raeburn to his wife Ann, but the tradition that the painter presented it to her as a birthday surprise seems questionable.

➠ *Right Dean Park Crescent leads to Dean Street.*

Dean Street was built up on its north side by 1813 and may be the first of the Raeburn Estate's streets to have been completed. William Bryce is believed to have been responsible for some of Dean Street's architecture, the exquisite detailing of which repays close examination.

Raeburn Street, *second left,* originally called Hermitage Place, was closed nightly as is evidenced by gate piers at both entrances. Although the street is only built up on one side, its pedimented central house provides it with Classical grandeur.

Raeburn Place, *right,* is another early development, 1814–25, with tenements at its east end; more attractive villas are found at the west end.

Deanhaugh Street, *ahead,* marks the commercial centre of Stockbridge. Architecturally it is still dominated by the tower of the former Free Church, the rest of which was demolished in 1980.

➠ *From the street's south end, cross the Stock Bridge. First left Hamilton Place (the Raeburn Estate has now been left).*

Until 1817 the Stockbridge Mills occupied the east bank of the river just north of the bridge, but otherwise, apart from a few scattered houses, rurality prevailed. St Stephen's Place (originally Market Place), *first right,* marks part of the site of

Stockbridge Market, 1825–1906; only its entrances have survived (the best of which is at the far end of St Stephen's Place).

➠ *Follow Hamilton Place northward. First left Dean Bank Lane. Firt left Saxe-Coburg Place.*

Saxe-Coburg Place was planned as a rectangle by James Milne in 1821, but when the site was taken over in 1828 its north–west range was converted to a crescent and never completed. However, the longer ranges, apart from the houses at their south ends, survive basically as Milne had designed them.

➠ *From the north-east corner of Saxe-Coburg Place, follow Gabriels Road northward to Glenogle Road.*

From the north side of Glenogle Road a series of short streets of the 1860s faced by a footpath lead to the Water of Leith. Collectively they are referred to as 'The Colonies', as it was here that colonial labourers had lodged while working on the construction of the New Town. As may be expected, the houses are now most desirable, particularly those overlooking the river at the north end of each street.

➠ *Follow Glenogle Road eastward. If visiting the Royal Botanic Garden, left Brandon Terrace. First left Inverleith Row leads to the garden's east entrance, left.*

➠ *Alternatively, if proceeding directly to the Northern New Town from Glenogle Road, right Brandon Street.*

Location 8   Royal Botanic Garden

Inverleith Row

❖ Open daily March, April, September and October 10am to 6pm, May to August 10am to 8pm, November to February 10am to 4pm. ❖ Admission free.

Covering 288 acres (25 ha), Edinburgh's Botanic Garden is almost exactly one-quarter the size of Kew's, near London, and as at Kew there is no internal transport. Formerly located in Leith Walk, the garden was transferred here 1822–24, but had its origins in a tiny physic garden established in 1670 near Holyrood. Near the west entrance, Inverleith House, a rather dour late 18th-century mansion, was incorporated in the grounds in 1876. Now used for temporary exhibitions, it became the first home of the Scottish National Gallery of Modern Art 1960–84. Around the house, Britain's largest collection of rhododendrons is particularly spectacular in March and April.

The garden's most important group of buildings lies in the north-east corner. A 200-year-old palm tree from the West Indies can be seen in the New Palm House of 1856; housed within the new glasshouses, built in 1967, are rare varieties of exotic orchids.

Plant collector George Forrest returned to Edinburgh with numerous specimens from his several expeditions to China made between 1904 and 1932. Partly due to his efforts, the most comprehensive collection of plants from China outside that country can be seen in the recently created Chinese Garden.

➠ *Exit from the Royal Botanic Garden by the Inverleith Row gate (there is an alternative gate to the east side of the garden from Aboretum Place). Inverleith Row crosses the Water of Leith. First right Brandon Terrace leads to Brandon Street. First right Henderson Row. Fourth left Clarence Street. First left St Stephen Street leads to St Vincent Street.*

Facing the long vista beginning with St Vincent Street, the church of St Stephen, originally destined for the west side of Royal Circus, was built by William Playfair, 1827–28. Playfair's favoured Grecian style is evident but he added some Baroque touches.

Surprisingly, another much smaller church, the Gothic Revival St Vincent, built in 1857, faces St Stephen from the opposite side of the same street.

➠ *Continue southward. First right North East Circus Place leads to Royal Circus.*

Location 9   Northern New Town

The grandeur of Royal Circus confirms that Stockbridge has been left for Edinburgh's Northern New Town, which stretches eastward, following the north sides of Heriot Row, Abercromby Place and Albany Street, thus running parallel with the First New Town development. As the scheme keeps to the steep north slope of the escarpment, the views are southward towards the Firth of Forth rather than northward towards Old Town and the castle. Robert Reid and William Sibbald laid out the street grid in 1802, closing its main axis, Great King Street, at each end with a garden square, reminiscent of Craig's treatment of George Street. Unlike many houses in other parts of Edinburgh's New Town, few here have suffered from alterations to their Georgian facades. Due to the slope, the north/south streets gain a picturesque quality, while grandeur is left to the main east/west streets, plus Royal Circus and Drummond Place.

Location 10   Royal Circus

Playfair designed Royal Circus in 1820, and it was built by 1823. An east/west road through the middle of the circus, continuing the Great King Street axis, had been proposed so that disturbance to residents by through traffic would be minimised, but the lie of the land proved too difficult for this. Playfair's solution was to maintain symmetry by creating two entrances on the east side and dropping

the central road diagonally north-westward in a serpentine manner. Houses on
the north and south sides form two separate crescents, but although their ground
levels vary significantly, none is stepped; Playfair has succeeded in making a virtue
out of a necessity by employing the varying gradients to add a picturesque quality
that would have been impossible with a flat site.

➠ *Return through North East Circus Place to St Vincent Street, right.*

From here Great King Street stretches eastward through the trees of Drummond
Place to London Street. The three linked thoroughfares were designed by Robert
Reid and built early in the 19th century. Before the trees in Royal Circus and
Drummond Place had matured, an impression of one grand avenue could be
gained.

➠ *Follow Howe Street southward from St Vincent Street.*

Howe Street was originally the main Edinburgh/Stockbridge road, which is why
so many shops were incorporated in the ground floors of the tenements when
they were built in 1809. Most of their fronts have survived with the original
pilasters intact.

➠ *Continue uphill to Heriot Row, second left.*

Heriot Row, completed in 1808, comprises two terraces, from both of which
there are open views across Queen Street Gardens, thus ensuring their popularity.
Reid was again the architect, but in 1864 the entire west terrace was given a third
storey between its centrepiece and the end pavilions, and from then on further
alterations have detracted from the original scheme.

Robert Louis Stevenson lived at No 17 (in the eastern terrace, left) from 1857 to
1880. A brass plaque on the gate is inscribed with his charming poem for children, *The Lamplighter*.

➠ *Return westward and continue to Darnaway Street, which leads to Moray Place.*

Location 11   Moray Estate

In 1782 the 9th Earl of Moray purchased a 13 acre (5.3 ha) estate; his son, the
10th Earl, decided in 1822 to develop it as the third sector of Edinburgh's New
Town, and James Gillespie Graham was appointed architect. Not only did the
land slope towards the ravine of the Water of Leith, it was also basically a diagonal
strip. To overcome this, Gillespie's layout primarily comprised a crescent, an oval
and a polygon, linked by two short sections of Great Stuart Street. For his work,
which included detailed drawings, Graham was paid a total fee of five guineas!
Moray, a famously careful Scot, also tied up purchasers legally to ensure that the

expense of the streets, pavements, sewage, boundary walls and gardens would be their collective responsibility. In spite of these clauses, the estate was a great success, both environmentally and financially. No other sector of New Town was completed that would so precisely match the architect's original intentions. Lord Moray himself decided to live at No. 28.

Although Moray Place is 12-sided, the visitor is only able to view any two of them at a time. Every other side has a pedimented centrepiece, its columns being repeated in pairs at each end, providing a palatial frontage.

⇢ *Great Stuart Place leads from the south-west quadrant of Moray Place to the oval Ainslie Place, which the same thoroughfare links with Randolph Crescent, left. First left Queensferry Street leads to Princes Street.*

Forth Rail Bridge

Firth of Forth

At the west end of the Firth of Forth, many formerly independent villages have been swallowed up by Edinburgh, some of them fairly recently; however, vestiges of their seafaring individuality have survived, presenting a marine contrast with the city itself. Paramount are South Queensferry, dramatically flanked by the two great Forth bridges, and Leith, which has recently added the Royal Yacht *Britannia* to its attractions. All can be reached by public transport, and an economically-priced ticket valid for one day permits unlimited bus travel between them.

Leith

Direct buses leave Edinburgh from Waverley Bridge to *Britannia*, returning via central Leith. Between its launching in 1953 and decommissioning in 1997, the Royal Yacht *Britannia* cruised over one million miles on 968 royal and official visits. Leith's historic port has been selected as its final home and the yacht is now open to the public as a museum. ❖ Open daily March to October 10.30am to 4.30pm, November to February 11.30am to 4.30pm. ❖ Admission charge. Highlights for most are the private rooms of the Queen and the Duke of Edinburgh, and the Dining Room, in which numerous heads of state have attended glittering functions.

In the town's centre, the comparatively recent proliferation of bars and restaurants along Shore, overlooking the Water of Leith, has resulted in the area becoming a major tourist attraction, particularly at weekends and during the Festival in August. Much infilling of derelict sites still has to be done, but the destruction of Leith's ancient buildings has at last been halted. Surviving buildings of architectural interest include the Custom House in Commercial Street, Lamb's House in Burgess Street and late-Georgian houses in Bernard and Constitution streets.

Newhaven

Virtually a suburb of Leith, Newhaven's small harbour, faced by its lighthouse, is a picturesque tourist attraction. Fishing was once an important industry, and old photos depict fishwives in local dress; memorabilia from this period can be seen in the Newhaven Heritage Museum. ❖ Open daily 12pm to 5pm. ❖ Admission free.

South Queensferry

Queensferry is unofficially known as South Queensferry simply to distinguish it from the other Queensferry on the north side of the Firth of Forth. Its name commemorates the many ferry crossings made by Queen Margaret from

Britannia

Edinburgh Castle to her palace at Dunfermline in the 11th century. The ferry service continued even after the Forth Rail Bridge opened to the east of the town in 1890. Sir John Fowler (who also constructed London's Metropolitan and District underground lines) and Benjamin Baker were responsible for its construction. To the west, and ensuring the demise of the ferry, the Forth Road Bridge opened in 1964. Pedestrians may cross its 1.5-mile footpath to Fife, enjoying sensational views of the railway bridge on route. Although built in completely different styles, and separated by seventy-four years, each bridge serves as a perfect visual foil for the other. Visitors to South Queensferry should not ignore the narrow High Street, with its appealing blend of primarily Georgian and Victorian houses and the Tolbooth Tower, which dates from the 12th century. ❖ At No. 53, Queensferry Museum is open Thursday to Monday 10am to 1pm and 2.15pm to 5pm. ❖ Admission free. The part 17th-century Hawes Inn makes an attractive lunchbreak venue.

Cramond

There are direct buses from Edinburgh to Cramond, but from Queensferry a change must be made at Barnton. Although now quite extensive, Cramond's visitor attractions all lie close to the breakwater, where the River Almond meets the sea. A popular walk follows its east bank, from where pleasure craft can usually be observed. Overlooking the scene, the core of the picturesque Cramond Inn was built in 1670. A short distance to the south, off Cramond Glebe Road, Cramond Kirk was built in the 17th century on the site of a medieval church, which itself occupied part of the site of a Roman fort. To the east, the central, crowstepped block of Cramond House was built around 1680. Towards the sea, Cramond Tower, a ruinous, probably late 15th-century tower house, formed part of a residence owned by the bishops of Dunkeld. At low tide, it is possible to walk along the top of the breakwater to the uninhabited Cramond Island. Lying a mile east of Cramond, with grounds overlooking the Firth of Forth, Lauriston Castle retains its original late 16th-century tower house, but the remainder is the 1827 Jacobean Revival work of William Burn. In 1926, the Reid family, who had lived at Lauriston since 1902, presented the house, with its collection of antiques, to the nation. The superb interiors are among Britain's finest Edwardian examples. ❖ Open April to October, Saturday to Thursday 11am to 5pm; November to March, Saturday and Sunday 2pm to 4pm. ❖ Admission charge.

INDEX OF LOCATIONS